The Abbasid House of Wisdom

This volume examines the library of the Abbasid caliphs, known as "The House of Wisdom" ("Bayt al-Hikma"), exploring how this important institution has been misconceived by scholars.

This book places the palace library within the framework of the multifaceted cultural and scientific activities in the era of the caliphs, Harun al-Rashid and al-Ma'mun, generally regarded as the Golden Age of Islamic civilization. The author studies the first references to the House of Wisdom in European sources and shows how misconceptions arose because of incorrect translations of Arabic manuscripts and also because of how scholars overlooked the historical context of the library in ways that reflected their own cultural and national ambitions.

The Abbasid House of Wisdom is perfect for scholars, students, and the wider public interested in the scientific and cultural activities of the Islamic Golden Age.

Ekmeleddin Ihsanoğlu is a Turkish scholar and diplomat and a pioneer of studies of Ottoman Science and the history of institutions of learning. He was the founder and chair of the first Department of the History of Science in Turkey at the University of Istanbul, the IRCICA, the Turkish Society for the History of Science, and president of the International Union of History and Philosophy of Science from 2001 to 2005. He is editor and co-author of many volumes, including 18 volumes of History of Ottoman Science Literature, and laureate of Alexandre Koyré Medal.

The Abbasid House of Wisdom
Between Myth and Reality

Ekmeleddin Ihsanoğlu

LONDON AND NEW YORK

First published 2023
by Routledge
4 Park Square, Milton Park, Abingdon, Oxon OX14 4RN

and by Routledge
605 Third Avenue, New York, NY 10158

Routledge is an imprint of the Taylor & Francis Group, an informa business

© 2023 Ekmeleddin Ihsanoğlu

The right of Ekmeleddin Ihsanoğlu to be identified as author of this work has been asserted in accordance with sections 77 and 78 of the Copyright, Designs and Patents Act 1988.

All rights reserved. No part of this book may be reprinted or reproduced or utilised in any form or by any electronic, mechanical, or other means, now known or hereafter invented, including photocopying and recording, or in any information storage or retrieval system, without permission in writing from the publishers.

Trademark notice: Product or corporate names may be trademarks or registered trademarks, and are used only for identification and explanation without intent to infringe.

British Library Cataloguing-in-Publication Data
A catalogue record for this book is available from the British Library

Library of Congress Cataloging-in-Publication Data
A catalog record has been requested for this book

ISBN: 978-1-032-34745-5 (hbk)
ISBN: 978-1-032-34748-6 (pbk)
ISBN: 978-1-003-32367-9 (ebk)

DOI: 10.4324/9781003323679

Typeset in Times New Roman
by codeMantra

Contents

Abbreviations vii
Preface ix
Acknowledgments xiii

PART I: Baghdad and the Rise of Interest in Foreign Sciences   1
   A *Revisiting the Abbasid House of Wisdom 8*
   B *Short Note on the Proposed Origins of*
      the House of Wisdom 10

PART II: Creating A Myth   14

PART III: Dissecting the Myth   25
   A *Bayt al-Hikma and Translation Movement 28*
   B *Bayt al-Hikma as a University 31*

PART IV: What to Call a Library in Arabic?   34

PART V: What Was the Abbasid Caliph's Library Called?   39

PART VI: Was the House of Science an Arena for Debates?   50

PART VII: What Was the Reality?   56
   A *The Origin of Book Collections 59*
   B *Patronage Associated with the Library 60*
   C *The Library and Greek Books 61*
   D *Abbasid Caliphal Library and Persian*
      Royal Libraries 64

PART VIII: What Happened to the House of Wisdom?   **68**

PART IX: The Impact   **72**

PART X: Concluding Remarks   **78**

Bibliography   81
Index   89

Abbreviations

AN. I: Al-Nadim's The Fihrist Al-Furqan Edition Vol: 1
AN. II: Al-Nadim's The Fihrist Al-Furqan Edition Vol: 2
Dodge: Bayard Dodge, The Fihrist of Al-Nadim:
               A Tenth-Century Survey of Muslim Culture
Ibn Juljul: Ibn Juljul al-Andalusi, Tabaqat al-'Atibba
Al-Qifti: Al-Qifti's Tarih al-Hukama
Rosenfeld-
Ihsanoglu: Rosenfeld, Boris A., Ihsanoglu,
               Ekmeleddin, Mathematicians,
               astronomers, and other scholars of
               Islamic civilization and their works
               (7th–19th c.), IRCICA Publication
EI^2:   Encyclopedia of Islam, 2nd Edition
EI^3:   Encyclopedia of Islam, 3rd Edition

Preface

The ninth-century Abbasid palace library known as the House of Wisdom has attracted the attention of generations of scholars from the end of the nineteenth century until today. The transformation of this institution from a palace library into a nineteenth-century modern European academy or fully-fledged modern-day university has had a very interesting journey.

In this book, we shall take up the few accounts in the classical Arabic sources and references in the biographies of the scholars associated with this library and evaluate how they were turned into a myth. Some innocent errors, the shifting of a word's meaning during translation, the imagination of those dealing with the subject, and also emotional and nationalist aspirations paved the way for the birth of this myth.

The early studies conducted by pioneering orientalists reveal that the first examples of the confusion related to Bayt al-Hikma resulted from the problems of editing Arabic manuscripts or translating specific Arabic words and terms that had no standard equivalents in the European languages. At the turn of the twentieth century Bayt al-Hikma was transformed into an active institution of scientific pursuit including a library and observatory. As will be explained under Part II, a PhD dissertation came to the conclusion that

> the "House of Wisdom" appears to have been the university of Baghdad with its distinguished performance, library and observatory ... [it] may justly claim the honor of having been the first university of both the medieval and the modern world; for it bore the torch aloft long before Bologna, Paris, Prague, Oxford and Cambridge ...

At the turn of the twenty-first century, a new episode in the long history of the creation of this myth was a new claim that Bayt al-Hikma had "roots that go deep in history; that is to say in the heritage of ancient Iraq from the days of the Sumerians, the Babylonians and the Assyrians."

In the last decades, an observed increase of interest among wide segments of western readership for the scientific achievements and accomplishments in the history of Muslim world, as well as the contributions of Muslim scholars and philosophers to the making of the Western civilization, has propelled popular publications addressed to a wide range of readership. These publications aimed to introduce the Abbasid House of Wisdom as a pivot behind the Golden Age of the Islamic civilization that epitomized the splendid glory of the past. However, these new publications were based on previous ones produced by generations of scholars where limited information in few primary sources regarding this palace library turned out, in the hands of Western and Muslim scholars, to be an endless source of inspiration which led to the creation of a myth of an Abbasid academy of sciences similar to European ones and a full-fledged modern university.

The main difficulty in comprehending the nature of the Abbasid palace library, at times referred to as "Khizanat al-Hikma" (Repository of Wisdom) and at others as "Bayt al-Hikma" (House of Wisdom), is how to situate this library within the overall framework of the multifaceted cultural and scientific activities in the era of the two caliphs Harun al-Rashid and al-Ma'mun, generally known as the golden age of the Islamic civilization. What is certain about these activities is that they were, in the main, held under caliphal patronage and their entourage. Indeed, the poets, the literary figures, religious scholars, physicians, astronomers, and astrologers who belonged to different religions and hailed from varied origins exercised their activities under the patronage of the caliph and with his financial support.

Careful and critical examination of the available information provided by the primary sources that have reached us has undoubtedly clarified many misunderstandings and helped to undo the fanciful portrait of the House of Wisdom. As for the claims that all these varied activities used to take place within the House of Wisdom and inside its "specialized departments", we have clearly shown that this claim has no historical support.

There are certain specific figures as mentioned by the primary sources who were attached to the Palace library and who did work there officially. They, however few, are quite limited in number, but they stand as a proof to the existence of some mode of organized institutional work within the palace library that goes beyond the mere collection and preservation of books and encompasses other activities such as authoring, translating, and copying books.

By researching how the myth of the House of Wisdom was created and disseminated, we endeavored to dissect the fanciful image and tried to construct a real depiction of the ninth century caliphal library, in accordance with the accounts available in primary sources.

This study shows that scholars who were addressing the history of the House of Wisdom overlooked the historical context and that they were reading modern institutions into classical texts, idealizing its structure and functioning in a way that reflected their own emotional aspirations and national ambitions.

This study also dismisses many claims and propositions generated and continued by generations of scholars that became *a priori* self-evident propositions. It also shows how elitist institutions, if they disregard the sensitivities of the public and harbored heterodox interests, would end up losing their sustainability.

Having proved that the myth which was created no longer stands in the face of reality, one cautionary remark is to admit that the mythical image of the House of Wisdom developed over many years has become well established to the extent that the bare reality stands as an unwelcome stranger while the myth seems a household acquaintance.

İstanbul, 23.12.2021
E. Ihsanoglu

Acknowledgments

This book is the first offspring came through several decades of ongoing research on the development of institutions of learning in Islam which covers the classic period from the eighth to the sixteenth century. Concerning this book on the history of the Abbasid House of Wisdom, I would like to express my thanks to my former colleague Dr. Yümna Özer from IRCICA for her contribution at the first stages of the project.

I would like to acknowledge with appreciation the kind hospitality of Prof. Hans G. Mayer during my sojourn in Ludwig-Maximilian University in Munich in 2003, where I enjoyed thought-provoking discussions with brilliant graduate students of Institut für Geschichte und Kultur des Nahen Orients sowie Turkologie during the hauptseminar: Institutions of Learning in Islam. I also recall the fruitful exchange of views on early Abbasid texts with late Prof. Rainer Degen of the "Institut für Semitistik" of Munich University.

Finally, I must express my gratitude to Oğuz Kaan Pehlivan, whose diligent and studios help made my manuscript find its way to the printer.

Part I Baghdad and the Rise of Interest in Foreign Sciences

Baghdad, the capital of the "Abbasid Caliphate", was established after a careful search for the most suitable place to establish as the basis of the new administration and the new army. Al-Mansur (754–775), the second Abbasid Caliph, selected a fertile and strategically convenient place on the main routes of communications with various parts of the empire.[1] The historical growth of Baghdad, beginning with a magnificent, round city constructed by al-Mansur in 145/762, suggests a rather different type of urban development. The round city, or Madinat al-Salam (the city of peace), as it was also called, was not a prefabricated military camp given permanency by a growing sedentary environment, but rather the product of consummate planning and execution.[2]

The advent of Islam and the Arab conquests brought to an end the old divisions that separated the civilized world for a millennium since the time of Alexander the Great. Egypt and the fertile crescent were united with Persia, Central Asia, and India under central political authority based in Baghdad. This led to the free flow of goods, knowledge, and ideas. It was the agricultural revolution of the first centuries after the Arab conquest that provided much of the wealth of the early empire and benefited all social strata.[3]

The earliest settlers of Baghdad were undoubtedly the followers and supporters of the caliph. They were the Abbasid family, the companions, the client (Mawali), the commanders, the army, and the masses. The quick growth of the population and of economic activity led to the expansion of a Baghdad as a whole, until it became the greatest city in the empire and the largest in the world. The capital of the Abbasid Empire was a real metropolis, and better representative of the Islamic Empire than semi-nomadic Medina or quasi-Byzantine Damascus. Arabic, Aramaic, Persian, and Turkish cultures were living together as early as its foundation, and the scantiness of the Greco-Byzantine

DOI: 10.4324/9781003323679-1

elements was compensated for by the active translation of the Greek intellectual heritage into Arabic.[4]

The population was nevertheless linked together by the common bonds of the Arabic language, the Islamic religion, and their allegiance to the caliph who stood above racial divisions. The army and the officials formed the majority of the population of early Baghdad as they did in the *amsar* (garrison towns); but whereas the *amsar* were dominated by a population of almost purely Arabic nomadic stock whose relations with the government were not always smooth, the population of early Baghdad had good relations with the ruling Abbasid Caliphs. The non-Arab elements were many, but the caliph's support of the nomadic culture and the Arabs created a balance and a peaceful process of establishing a cosmopolitan civilization into which were integrated the numerous different cultures that already existed in the Middle East.[5]

Baghdad, as Ira M. Lapidus observes, was the product of upheavals, population movements, economic changes, and conversions of the preceding century; it became the home of a new, heterogeneous, and cosmopolitan Middle Eastern society. Under the Abbasids the empire no longer belonged to the Arabs, though they had conquered its territories, but to all those peoples who would share in Islam and in the emerging networks of political, social, economic, and cultural loyalties which defined a new cosmopolitan Middle Eastern society. The Abbasids continued the Umayyad effort to centralize political power in the hands of the caliph and the ruling elite.

Many of the scribes in the expanding Abbasid bureaucracy were Persians from Khurasan, who had begun to enter the central government under the late Umayyads. Nestorian Christians were powerfully represented, while certain smaller minorities such as Jews were active in tax and banking activities. Under the Caliphs al-Mahdi (r. 775–785) and Harun al-Rashid (r. 786–809), the members of the Barmakid family were actively engaged in bureaucracy. The Barmakids who were often described as Persian but were more precisely central Asian Iranian, descended from Buddhist priesthoods of the city of Balkh. Shortly after the foundation of Baghdad, Khalid al-Barmaki became the chief minister for al-Mansur. They played an outstanding role in the first half of the Abbasid rule. Though powerful, the Barmakids were not chiefs of the whole administration. The empire was tolerant and inclusive rather than monolithic.[6]

The upper class of Abbasid society was formed by a coalition of provincial and capital city elites, who agreed on a common concept of the dynasty and the purposes of political power and who were organized

Baghdad and the Rise of Interest in Foreign Sciences 3

through bureaucratic and other political institutions to impose their rule on the population of the empire. The bureaucracy mobilized the skills and social influence of prominent persons throughout the empire and put these assets at the disposal of Baghdad.[7]

Arabic was the mother tongue of the Arabs, the religious language of the Muslims, and the cultural instrument of the scholars who began to flock to the flourishing new imperial capital, enjoying the freedom of thought and non-interference of the state. Those scholars were scattered in the various quarters of the city, and they did not have one academic center, but preferred to teach in the mosques.

The early Abbasid Caliphs endeavored to encourage Arabic culture and chose Arabic scholars to educate their sons. They encouraged the collecting of pre-Islamic Arabic poetry as well as the translation into Arabic of Greek and Indian works in medicine, astronomy, geometry, and mathematics. Many commanders and notables shared with the caliphs in their interests and thereby aided in establishing Arabic firmly in the new city as well as in the empire.[8]

There were no formal institutions of learning. Instead, intellectual activities were conducted in various places. Mosques were the seat of major scholarly and educational endeavors in the field of religious studies while most literary and scientific activities that enlisted the interest of the caliphs, including different aspects of writing and translation, were undertaken around the caliph's court. No doubt, the homes of scholars and literati were the first incubators of their activities.

The court of the caliphs and the administrative and political elite contributed especially to Islamic art, architecture, philosophy, science, and Iranian and Hellenistic forms of literatures in Arabic. The court and the aristocratic milieu, while accepting the Islamic identity, stressed the aspects of belles-lettres, science, and philosophy to help define the authority of the regime and the legitimacy of the ruling classes. A common culture, shared values, symbols, and ideas were essential for the functioning of this elite. A literary and philosophic culture was needed to present a vision of the universe with a preeminent role given to the state and the ruler in the divine plan and in the functioning of human society, and a concept of the nature of the human beings and their destiny in this world and the next.

Thus, the Abbasid dynasty patronized Arabic poetry and the translation into Arabic of Iranian literary classics including works of history, polite literature, fables, political precepts and manuals of protocol, behavior for scribes, and the mythic and scientific lore of Persia and India. Similarly, Syriac and Greek classics in science, medicine, and philosophy were translated into Arabic.[9] So the court served to propagate a pre-Islamic concept of the ruler and the empire. Interest in the secular aspects of Arabic literature, Persian Adab, and Hellenistic philosophies and sciences signified the appropriation of a cultural heritage which could be used to legitimize caliphal rule. They provided, in the Arabic case, an ethnic concept of political leadership, in the Persian case, a continuation of the heritage of ancient Middle Eastern kings, and in the Hellenistic case, a concept of the structure of the universe itself, in philosophic and scientific form, as the ultimate justification for imperial rule. The patronage of these several literatures implied ultimately that the caliph, though a Muslim ruler, was legitimized in non-Islamic cultural terms going back to the heritage of the ancient Middle East.[10]

Urban Islamic religious culture was ultimately the amalgamation of different orientations including Qur'anic exegesis, hadith (prophetic traditions), law, theology, mystical discourse, and the Shi'ite concept of Imamate. Meanwhile the heritage of Greece and Iran as well as Arabia was being incorporated into Islam. The historical religions of the Middle East were recast into a new, high cultural monotheistic vision.[11] In the theological field some Muslim scholars came to realize that Greek methods of argumentation were a useful weapon against both Muslim opponents and non-Muslims.[12]

During this period, the sciences of the ancients ('ulum al-'awa'il) also called foreign sciences (al-'ulum al-dakhila), rational or intellectual sciences (al-'ulum al'aqliyya), or philosophical sciences (al-'ulum al-falsafiyya, or al-'ulum al-hikamiyya or what is shortly known as al-hikma/wisdom) were transmitted from antiquity and formed an integral part of the new encyclopedia of knowledge. The integration of these sciences in the epistemological and educational structure was a long process which started in this era and was achieved in steps.

The diversification of literary and scholarly interests that developed in the early Abbasid era had its impact on wider segments of society. The introduction of paper as a writing material in the lands of the Abbasid Caliphate, after the Talas Battle took place in Taraz (in today's Kazakhstan) between the Muslim and the Chinese armies (Tang dynasty) in 134/751, brought the art of papermaking to Samarkand from where it spread shortly after to the capital city of Baghdad and to the rest of the Muslim world. The establishment of the first paper mill in Baghdad around 795 transformed Abbasid culture from an oral tradition to a bookish culture. This revolutionary process in producing inexpensive books helped the credibility of the earlier oral tradition of Arabic and Islamic tradition and also helped the dissemination of these sciences as well as the foreign sciences to a larger audience of learned people. Thus, it was not only the limited circle of the caliph's courtiers that admired and developed an affinity to foreign sciences but also a wider social milieu that developed a taste and interest in these sciences as a mark of civilized behavior. Acquiring and cultivating the knowledge of foreign sciences became a prerequisite for becoming an intellectual.

After the second/eighth century and until the Mongol invasion, Baghdad was the center where arts and sciences were sought. In addition to some clues in the primary sources that enlighten certain aspects of intellectuality in early Abbasid period, we know also cultural image of Abbasid life mirrored in the partly fanciful tale of Arabian Nights where scholars, as well as simple people such as the chatterbox barber, are portrayed as an astrologer and learned in alchemy and white magic, syntax, grammar and lexicology, the arts of logic, rhetoric and elocution, mathematics, arithmetic and algebra, astronomy, astromancy and geometry, theology, traditions of the prophet, and commentaries of the Quran.[13]

And not only were men, scholars, and barbers expected to have an encyclopedic knowledge, but young and beautiful slave girls were also expected to be, or perhaps dreamt of, as mines of learning and wisdom. In the story of "Abu al-Hasan and his Slave Girl Tawaddud", the latter describes herself as one versed in syntax and poetry and jurisprudence and exegesis and philosophy, saying that

> I am skilled in music and the knowledge of the Divine ordinance and in arithmetic and geodesy and geometry and the fables of the ancients. I know the Sublime Qur'an by heart and have read it according to the seven, the ten and the fourteen modes. I know the number of its chapters and verses and sections and words ... I know the Holy Traditions ... and I have studied the exact sciences, geometry and philosophy and medicine and logic and rhetoric and composition; and I have learnt many things by rote and am passionately fond of poetry. I can play the lute ...[14]

These narratives imply the quality and amplitude of life in the city as well as the wide scope of scholars, combining interest and erudition in both indigenous Arabic and Islamic sciences, as well as in foreign sciences or the sciences of the ancients.

In previous studies, we have maintained that the classical sciences or sciences of the ancients *'ulum al-'awa'il* were first transferred through translations, encouraged by the help of official and semi-official patronage, personal intellectual inquiry, and exploration. This classical heritage became an integral part of knowledge, *'ilm,* as described theoretically in the epistemological models established by Muslim scholars, and as explicitly expressed in the different classifications of sciences and being an official component of teaching in some Muslim institutions of learning, including madrasas at a later stage. This process, which started with the personal interest of the Abbasid Caliphs in the eighth century, acquired an institutional character in the following centuries and found its formal shape in the fifteenth century, and by the sixteenth century it was well established in the Ottoman epoch.

Primary sources are unanimous on al-Ma'mun's interest in knowledge and scholarship. The lengthy narratives of his legal, theological, and intra- and interconfessional debates, and his knowledge of theology and the law, enabled him to participate in intellectual and religious discussions and reflect on his personal involvement in his milieu's scholarly debate. Out of genuine interest in scholarly matters, he held regular disputations in which literary, religious, theological, and philosophical issues were discussed. He not only encouraged research into ancient science and philosophy but also personally pursued research.[15] Al-Dinawari (d. 896) noted that al-Ma'mun excelled among the Abbasids in learning; he acquired a certain degree of knowledge about it and had an active interest in every branch of knowledge.[16] For example, he was involved extensively enough in astronomical calculations to verify, while in Damascus, conflicting observational results and to check the functioning of instruments for accurate measurement.

Meanwhile, it was in al-Ma'mun's era that a divide emerged between religiously motivated scholars and those who adopted Greek philosophy and its instruments of disputation. This divide was intensified by the enforcement of *mihna*/inquisition by Caliph al-Ma'mun as will be shown below.

In al-Ma'mun's (r. 813–833) attempt to consolidate his power, enforce his centralized administration and eventually get away with any legitimacy issues, he adopted what came to be known as *Mihna* (inquisition/ordeal). Al-Ma'mun's new policy was based on absolutist interpretation of Islam, with the caliph as the ultimate arbiter of dogmas. This unpredicted, strange move was completely against the current decentralization of religious authority that had been gaining momentum until al-Ma'mun's time. His policy when he returned from Merv to Baghdad in 819 was centered on controlling the religious discussions in the capital, and by extension in the Islamic world. A rising threat to his authority was that numerous religious scholars were perceived as the proper interpreters of Islam, thus taking power away from the central authority.[17]

Al-Ma'mun, in his adoption of the view of the "createdness of Qur'an", forced religious scholars to conform to this doctrine of the Mu'tazila, otherwise they would be persecuted, punished, imprisoned, and even killed. This doctrine implies that the Qur'an was a worldly object, and thus not itself part of the divine being. This was in contrast with the idea that the Qur'an was uncreated, in other words eternal, and an emanation of and part of the divine being.

The Mu'tazilites were heavily influenced by Greek philosophy. They insisted that the divine attributes such as knowledge (omniscience) had no-existence of any sort except in God's essence. It followed that the Qur'an, if it was uncreated, was some sort of eternal existence besides God's essence, and so an infringement of His unity and for this reason they insisted that it was created and not eternal; thus, it could be altered by the divinely inspired Imam.[18] On the other hand, the advocates of hadith stood in contrast to the idea that the Qur'an was created and they maintained that the Qur'an was not created and it was an emanation of and part of the divine being. This position practically meant also that revelation (including Qur'an and hadith) was above all human authority. They organized a separate movement under the leadership of Ahmed Ibn Hanbal (d. 241/855), in resistance to the inquisition put forth by al-Ma'mun.

Al-Ma'mun's policy toward createdness of the Qur'an widened the differences between the two forms of early Islamic culture and community: between the division of state and religious communities; between the court and urban *ulema;* between the cosmopolitan and religious forms of Islamic civilization. Al-Ma'mun declared himself as Imam al-Huda, the guide inspired by God, and the Caliph of God (*Khalifat Allah*).[19]

The term *Hikma* seems to have undergone a semantic evolution since it meant wisdom and classical sciences, which was then associated with "heretical" beliefs and came to refer to vulgarization of the teaching of the Isma'ili doctrine as such.[20] The *Durus al-hikma, sama' al-hikma or majalis al-hikma* as described by Qadi al-Nu'man (d. 974) were destined to diffuse the principles of Shi'ite (and Isma'ili) *fiqh*.[21] After al-Mutawakkil (r. 842–861) put an end to the inquisition (in 850), the term *"hikma"* started to imply heavy Mu'tazila or even Sh'ite connotations, and so the appellation was carefully avoided and *"Bayt al-Hikma's"* heirs or successors were named *"Dar al-'Ilm" (The House of Science/Knowledge).* Could it be also the reason why the Fatimid Caliph al-Hakim's *"Dar al-Hikma"*, an institution that oscillated between Sunni Islam and Isma'ili propaganda and was first named *"Dar al-Hikma"*, became known as also *"Dar al-'Ilm"* *(The House of Science/Knowledge)* in order to hide its Shi'te-Ismaili tendencies and enhance its Sunni facade?

It is against this diversified background that the Abbasid palace library was born and established and was attributed with different names and appellations. So, in revisiting the House of Wisdom in attempt to clarify the ambiguities and to correct the depiction of caliphal library, we should keep in mind this panoramic frame of the social and cultural factors in the capital of the Abbasid Empire.[22]

A Revisiting the Abbasid House of Wisdom

The emergence of institutions of learning and their continuation or decline will be better understood when they are considered in their sociocultural context. Elitist institutions only survive by royal patronage and seldom endure the demise of their patrons unless their foundations are in harmony with the social dynamics or are adequately endowed with the means of survival. Thus, the durability and sustenance of any institution will not depend on the patronage of its founder but on the stance of the society that it belongs to, its cultural mission and the need for the continuation of its mission, and the intellectual approach of its scholars and whether it is in harmony with the values of the society. Overlooking the historical context of these institutions, reading modern models into classical texts, and idealizing their structures and functions according to the ambition of the scholars who study them, can only serve to create more confusion in the objective rewriting of their history. The similarities between institutions belonging to consequent civilizations constitute another difficult aspect in the study of these institutions. Whether the new institutions were inspired or influenced by previous ones or emerged as a natural development in answer to certain demands and needs which led to their formation in such a way that they reflected similar characteristics that could be considered as the result of inspiration, imitation, or amelioration, are other interesting questions.

All these issues pose problems in studying these institutions and attempting to readdress and rewrite their history objectively. For scholars, this task will be more intriguing particularly in the absence of sufficient historical reports and narratives and due to the fragmented and scattered nature of the surviving accounts.

Readdressing and rectifying the image of any institution created by generations of scholars because of misunderstanding of certain texts or due to anachronistic, and historicist maladies is not an easy undertaking; the most difficult aspect of such reconsideration would be the lack of enthusiasm in welcoming the new realistic and rather modest results as compared to the established and glittering images.

The historiography of the Abbasid House of Wisdom (Bayt al-Hikma) seems to be a perfect example of all the above and more. The ninth-century palace library of the Abbasid Caliphs in Baghdad acquired a strange image during the twentieth century, because of the abovestated reasons and with additional exaggerated concerns due to national and emotional aspirations, which dominated a significant part of the scholarship.

The information related by historical sources about the palace library of the Abbasid Caliphs Harun al-Rashid (r. 786–809) and his son al-Ma'mun (r. 813–833) is very limited. This scanty information is scattered in historical sources and comprises few surviving anecdotes and bio-bibliographical notes. Among them are a few anecdotes relating to their reigns, in addition to some references provided by al-Nadim (d. 990) for the first time in his book *al-Fihrist*, which is the main source of our information on the cultural life in the early Abbasid period and includes extensive bibliographic information on written and translated Arabic works produced in this time. This and the later sources, which divulge some information, do not go beyond referring to the existence of a palace or court library during the reign of the two caliphs and a late reference to the reign of al-Mu'tadid (r. 892–902), and the names of some scholars who were associated with this library. The few lines in these sources somehow constituted an inexhaustible source for the imagination of some scholars and their farfetched assumptions. Later, the resulting picture of the Abbasid House of Wisdom as an "academy" comprising various departments, including a school or bureau of translation, an observatory, and others, was developed into the myth of the first "university" in history.

As we shall discuss and refute these baseless claims in detail and try to deconstruct this inflated image, it is essential to indicate the nature and context of the handful of historical references that turned out to be inexhaustible sources for this historical concoction. The surviving anecdotes and short references, which we shall quote later in detail, refer to the caliphal library using different wordings. The palace library was the repository or storehouse (khizana) or the house (bayt) of books of wisdom (hikma), a word which in this context denotes that the subjects of these books were primarily foreign sciences, that is, non-religious sciences introduced from Greek, Syriac, Indian, and Sassanian sources.

A careful examination of al-Nadim's few references clearly show that he refers to the palace library of the two caliphs with different combinations of the aforementioned words. It seems that some modern scholars have taken these variants as expressions of different institutions and the compound name "Bayt al-Hikma" was the appellation for a different institution which they thought was more than a palace library.

Modern scholars dealing with the different aspects of cultural life in the early Abbasid period tend to portray the court library known as the House of Wisdom as the pivot of all cultural and scholarly activities and religious and philosophical discussions, and they placed it in the middle of vehement controversy and depicted it as the arena of debates and disputations among the proponents and the opponents of al-Ma'mun's enforcement of the createdness of the Qur'an. This is one of many other aspects related to the false picture of the Abbasid House of Wisdom that this book will address.

This book presents an attempt to scrutinize the available sources and to assess them far from historicist and anachronistic approaches. It discusses how the inflated picture of the Abbasid House of Wisdom was drawn out of a misunderstanding of some terms and words, the idealization of certain aspects, and later how emotional and national inspirations completely distorted the ninth-century caliphal library through unreasonable concoctions. Meanwhile, it tries to contextualize the available historic accounts and scanty information in a straightforward narrative.

B Short Note on the Proposed Origins of the House of Wisdom

The theoretically plausible idea that the Abbasid institution called the House of Wisdom was inspired from Greek or Persian institutions is an independent issue of research that lies outside the scope of this study. However, in the context of this study, we will content ourselves with one broad remark to enable the reader to grasp the wider background of this institution.

Despite the scarcity of information, some modern scholars claimed that common features can be found between Hellenic Athenian, Ptolemaic, and Sassanid institutions of learning and those institutions which were developed by Muslims mainly in Baghdad and later in Cairo. According to this opinion, *"Hikma"* foundations display elements of similarity with some previous educational foundations, such as the philosophical schools in Athens, the Museum of Alexandria, and Jundishapur.[23] However, these scholars did not provide any convincing evidence in support of their opinion.

Islamic Hellenism was not solely the product of the conquests of Alexandria and Antioch; it derived largely from what was already present within the Sassanian realms.[24] It is also plausible that the Abbasid Caliph al-Ma'mun and Fatimid Caliph al-Hakim patterned their *Bayt al-Hikma* and *Dar al-Hikma* on the examples of Persian Jundishapur (Gundaysabur/Gondeshapur).[25] George Sarton (d. 1956) suggests that Jundishapur truly flourished under Nushirwan the Just (r. 531–579), after the expulsion of Nestorians from Edessa in 489 and the banishment of Neo-Platonists from Athens in 529.[26] It became one of the greatest cosmopolitan shelters for philosophy and science, be it Greek, Jewish, Christian, Hindu, and Persian.[27] Jundishapur's fame lies in its importance as a secular cultural center, reputed for its tradition of medicine, which was a source of inspiration for the intellectual activity in Islam.[28] Its role seems to have been more important for the transmission of knowledge than creative scientific activities.[29] No doubt that Jundishapur, through its physicians, was one of the main channels through which Greek science, medicine, and other sciences of the ancients were introduced into the Abbasid Empire. Jundishapur was not only a great *bimaristan* (shifakhane-hospital), it was also described as a center of medicine and philosophy, as well as a translation center where many Greek medical texts were transposed by physicians into Syriac. Many renowned physicians were gathered here, among them were members of the famous Bakhtishu family who had been Abbasid Court physicians for generations.

Notes

1 Salah Ahmed El-Ali, "The Foundation of Baghdad", in *The Islamic City A Colloquium*, edited by A. H. Hourani and S. M. Stern, published by Bruno Cassiran, Oxford University Press and University of Pennsylvania Press, 1970, p. 92
2 S. Lassner, "The Caliph's Personal Domain the City Plan of Baghdad Reexamined", in *The Islamic City A Colloquium*, edited by A. H. Hourani and S. M. Stern, published by Bruno Cassiran, Oxford University Press and University of Pennsylvania Press, 1970, pp. 103–107.
3 For social and cultural background of the Greek-Arabic translation movement, see D. Gutas, *Greek Thought, Arabic Culture, the Graeco-Arabic Translation Movement in Baghdad and Early Abbasid Society*, London, Routledge, 1998, pp. 11–16.
4 El-Ali, pp. 95–99, and p. 92–97; S. Lassner, pp. 103–107.
5 El-Ali, pp. 99–100.

6. Ira M. Lapidus, *A History of Islamic Societies*, Cambridge University Press, 1993, pp. 71–73; and Bernard Lewis, *The Middle East 2000 years of History*, Phoenix, 2001, pp. 77–78.
7. Lapidus, pp. 79–80.
8. El-Ali, p. 99.
9. Lapidus, pp. 82–83.
10. Ibid., p. 97.
11. Lapidus, 2020 edition, pp. 114–117.
12. William Montgomery Watt, *A Short History of Islam*, One World Publication, Oxford, 1996, p. 104.
13. Richard F. Burton, A plain and literal translation of the Arabian Nights entertainments now entitled The Book of the *Thousand Nights and a Night*, with introduction explanatory notes on the manners and customs of Moslem men and a terminal essay upon the history of the Nights, edited by Richard F. Burton, Benares, Kamashastra Society, 1885–1886, Vol. 1, p. 305
14. Ibid., "Tale of the Tailor", Vol. 5, pp. 193–194.
15. See summary given by Hayrettin Yücesoy, *The Messianic Beliefs & Imperial Politics in Medieval Islam, The Abbasid Caliphate in the Early Ninth Century*, The University of South Carolina Press, 2009, pp. 116–135.
16. Al-Dinawari, Al-Akhbar Al-Tiwal, p. 400–4001 (quoted in the Yücesoy's above mentioned study p. 116).
17. On this subject, see brief and balanced explanations, D. Gutas particularly Al-Ma'mun: Domestic and Foreign Policies and the Translation Movement, pp. 75–104.
18. W.M. Watt, pp. 111–116.
19. Ira M. Lapidus, *A History of Islamic Societies*, 3rd Edition, 2014, 6th print, 2020, pp. 104–105 and pp. 171–174.
20. A. M. Goichon, "Hikma", EI^2, pp. 377–378.
21. For Qadi al-Nu'man, Kitab al-Majalis, see Farhat Dachraoui, "Contribution a l'Histoire des Fatimides en Ifriqya", *Arabica Journal*, Vol. 8, 1961, p. 191.
22. Against this background of the struggle between Hadith people and the Mu'tazila, G. Makdisi built his theory of emergence of Madrasa institution. See George Makdisi, *The Rise of Colleges: Institutions of Learning in Islam and The West*, Edinburgh University Press, 1981. For critic of this theory and proposing a new approach on development of institutions of learning in Islam, see, Ekmeleddin Ihsanoglu, "Institutions of Science Education", in *Oxford Encyclopedia of Philosophy, Science and Technology in Islam*, Editor Ibrahim Kalın, Vol I, Oxford University Press, 2014, pp. 386–397; Ekmeleddin Ihsanoglu, "Il Ruolo Delle Istituzioni", In *Storia Della Scienza*, Vol. 3, Rome, Instituto Della Enciclopedia Italiana Fondata da Giovanni Treccani, 2002, pp. 110–139. For an enlarged text of this research see; Ekmeleddin Ihsanoglu, "Institutions of Learning in Islam During the Classical Period (Eighth to Sixteenth Centuries): A Critical Overview", *Edebiyattan Tıp Tarihine Uzun İnce Bir Yol: Festschrift in Honor of Nuran Yıldırım II, Journal of Turkish Studies / Türklük Bilgisi Araştırmaları*, Harvard University, Vol. 56, 2001.
23. Y. Eche, is one of the first scholars to advance these claims, Ibid., pp. 48–55.

Baghdad and the Rise of Interest in Foreign Sciences   13

24 Francis E. Peters, *The Harvest of Hellenism. A History of the Near East from Alexander the Great to the Triumph of Christianity.* New York, Simon & Shuster, 1972, p. 568.
25 Halm Heinz, *The Fatimids and Their Tradition of Learning*, London, I.B. Tauris, in association with the Institute of Ismaili Studies, 1997, p. 72–73; Aydın Sayılı, "Gondeshapur", In *Encyclopedia of Islam*, 2nd Edition, 1979, p. 1120; Ali Akbar Siassi, *L'Université de Gond-i Shapur et l'etendue de son rayonement*, in *Mélanges d'orientalisme offerts a Henri Massé*, Téhéran, Imprimerie de L'Université, 1963, p. 366–374.
26 George Sarton, *Introduction to the History of Science*, Vol. 1, Huntingdon (NY), Krieger, 1975, p. 417.
27 Ibid., pp. 417–435.
28 Sayılı, 1979, p. 1120.
29 Sarton, 1975, v.1, p. 419.

Part II Creating a Myth

The transformation of the Abbasid palace library, the House of Wisdom, into a nineteenth-century European academy or fully-fledged modern-day university, has had a very interesting adventure from the viewpoint of historiography. In the following pages, we shall take up the few accounts in the classical Arabic sources and references in the biographies of the scholars associated with this library, which were turned into a myth. Some innocent errors, the shifting of a word's meaning during translation, the imagination of those dealing with the subject, and also emotional and nationalist aspirations paved the way for the birth of this myth.

The early studies conducted by pioneering orientalists reveal that the first examples of the confusion related to Bayt al-Hikma resulted from the problems of editing Arabic manuscripts or translating specific Arabic words and terms that had no standard equivalents in the European languages. The first example of this confusion is found in Güstav Flügel's 1858 edition of the Ottoman bibliographer and polymath scholar Katib Çelebi's (d. 1657) hitherto unpublished famous encyclopedic bibliography *Kashf al-Zunun*. As quoted by Katib Çelebi from earlier biographic sources, the phrase about Salm, the head of the caliphal library known as the House of Wisdom, which in Arabic reads as "sahib Bayt al-Hikma", was translated to Latin as "libri beit el-hikmet auctor".[1] Here Salm was introduced as the author of a book entitled Bayt al-Hikma. However, this misunderstanding did not last long because Flügel, in publishing al-Nadim's *Fihrist* for the first time in 1871, corrected his mistake, and revised Bayt al-Hikma's translation as a library and the term *sahib* as a librarian "bibliothecario oder bibliothecae beit el-hikmet dictae praefecto".[2]

Moritz Steinschneider, in his leading study of the Arabic translations of Greek books, refers to Flügel's mistake [which follows suit in Suter's work][3] and confirms the information provided by al-Qifti

(d. 1248) and Katib Çelebi about Salm and translations made by him.[4] However, Steinschneider, while referring to Bayt al-Hikma as the "Institute of Sciences", unintentionally opens the door to a very wide and long chain of speculations about the nature of this library.

Another interesting example of shifting the meaning of a word can be seen in the translation of the word 'madrasa', the main educational institution of the Islamic world, to European languages. Italian priest Toderini Giambattista (d. 1799) in his book on Ottoman Culture *De La Litterature des Turcs* translates madrasa as "Academy". Meanwhile, German orientalist F. Wüstenfeld (d. 1899) who translated Ibn Schobba's (d. 1448) *Tabaqat al-Shafi'iyya* which documents the life's and works of early shafi'i scholars, also used the word "academy" as equivalent to madrasa.[5]

The minor shift in understanding and translation of available historical accounts have had serious effects on the building up of the image of the hitherto unknown institution called Bayt al-Hikma. Hence, Bayt al-Hikma came alive as a great institution of learning with multifarious functions in Carl Brockelmann's first edition of *Geschichte der Arabischen Literatur*.[6] First published in 1898, it would be for decades an indispensable reference for all scholars of Islamic and Arabic studies. In his account of the translation activity that was carried on during the reign of Abbasid Caliph al-Ma'mun, Brockelmann presented Bayt al-Hikma, which according to him was founded by the caliph, as an active institution of scientific pursuit including a library and an observatory headed by Salm who was practicing as translator from Persian to Arabic. Brockelmann repeats this version of Bayt al-Hikma in the 1937 edition of his *Geschichte der Arabischen Literatur*[7] "in Baghdad al-Ma'mun founded the Bayt al-Hikma which also housed a library and observatory". This statement constitutes the main source for the image of an institute of science that includes many subsidiary departments for different scientific pursuits. It is rather paradoxical to mention that it was Brockelmann in his other studies, who sufficed himself with the real identification of Bayt al-Hikma as a court library founded by al-Ma'mun where he treasured books of Islamic and foreign cultures.[8]

Brockelmann drew the information about the translation of books in the early Abbasid period from Steinschneider, who did not suggest any of the new elements put forward in the expanded image of the House of Wisdom. Since none of the few references in the primary sources, however slight, conjectured in this context, it may be concluded that the source of such an image was probably due to the misunderstanding and confusion of references about the scholars, who were under the patronage of al-Ma'mun and involved in the translation activities and the Shamsiyah observatory, as will be explained in more detail below.

It seems clear that in presenting his first version of Bayt al-Hikma, Brockelmann was under the influence of the model of European academies in general and the Berlin Academy in particular, the third major academy in Europe. As envisaged by Leibniz, the *societās* under the patronage of the Prussian Court would be composed of different departments, salas, laboratories, and an observatory, consequently rising to the peak of learned societies in Europe, and would stand alongside the Paris Academy.[9] Perhaps Brockelmann was inspired by the Berlin Academy which impelled him to read in the primary Arabic sources of the ninth-century Abbasid court library, a nineteenth-century European academy. This would be his source of inspiration, supposedly, an academy of the Abbasid court compared to the academy of the Prussian Court.

The year 1928, strangely enough, witnessed three publications related to the reign of al-Ma'mun and cultural life during his reign, with diverse references to the House of Wisdom showing the different motivations of the authors. The first publication of this year was a doctoral thesis titled *The Contribution of Arabs to Education* by a Palestinian student Khalil Totah at Columbia University.[10] He later published his thesis in Arabic in 1933.[11] The introductory remarks of this young scholar show how enthusiastic and emotional he was about the glory of Arabic civilization in its golden age and his aspirations for the future of public education in the "awakening Arab world". He presented the House of Wisdom as an institution of high education where mathematics, astronomy, and philosophy were studied. The astonishing aspect of Totah's account of Bayt al-Hikma was that while he quoted from the known primary sources correctly, his comments were totally baseless; so in the conclusion he makes the following strange remarks:

> In conclusion the "House of Wisdom" appears to have been the university of Baghdad with its distinguished performance, library and observatory... [it] may justly claim the honor of having been the first university of both the medieval and the modern world; for it bore the torch aloft long before Bologna, Paris, Prague, Oxford and Cambridge ...[12]

The second publication was a book in Arabic about the age of al-Ma'mun ('Asr al-Ma'mun) written by Dr. Ahmad Farid Rifa'i a

Creating a Myth 17

graduate of the Egyptian University.[13] The book is a compilation from a number of chronicles and lectures of his Egyptian and European professors at the university. Despite his reference to Totah's book published earlier in the same year, he does not share any of unbiased exaggerations related to the House of Wisdom, which he refers to as the library of the "Ma'munian state".[14]

The third book published in this year presents new claims to the baseless image of Bayt al-Hikma. The construed image of Bayt al-Hikma, closely related to the European academy model, reached its maturity by acquiring a fixed date of establishment and the addition of a school of translation to its elaborate functions. Max Meyerhof (d. 1945), a German ophthalmologist living in Cairo, became interested in the history of his profession and published the original text and the English translation of the *Book of the Translations of Ten Treatises on the Eye* ascribed to Abbasid physician and translator Hunayn Ibn Ishaq (809–877). In his introduction, Meyerhof fixed the date of the establishment of Bayt al-Hikma as 830:

> .... The caliph who appointed him [Hunain Ibn Ishaq] as a kind of superintendent to his "library-academy" which he founded in Baghdad in 830 A.D., under the name of Bayt al-Hikma (House of Wisdom) ... A staff of young translators was employed in this institution in making translations from Greek into Syriac and later into Arabic ....[15]

Thus, he portrays the House of Wisdom as the caliph's translation school where Hunayn has trained his pupils.[16] It is clear that Meyerhof misunderstood the scattered references in the primary sources related to the biography of Hunayn Ibn Ishaq and added a school of translation to the "academy-library".

Two years later, Meyerhof in a famous article titled "From Alexandria to Baghdad" repeated his assertion that the Bayt al-Hikma was established by al-Ma'mun in 830. He also maintained that it was first headed by Yuhanna Ibn Masawayh who was Hunayn's teacher, but this time he claims that Hunayn Ibn Ishaq was appointed to the head of "this school" by the Caliph al-Mutawakkil after 25 years of Ibn Masawaih's leadership.[17]

It is obvious that Meyerhof thought that the positions of the director (sahib) of Bayt al-Hikma and the person who was in charge of the translations *(amin)* were the same; however, this was not the case. A careful examination of the sources at hand reveals that there is no mention of Yuhanna Ibn Masawayh or Hunayn's appointment as the director of

Bayt al-Hikma, but there is a clear reference to their being in charge of translations as (amin). It is reported that Yuhanna Ibn Masawayh was put in charge of translations by Harun al Rashed,[18] whereas Hunayn Ibn Ishaq was appointed to this task by al-Mutawakkil.[19] It is also quoted that as a young man he was asked by al-Ma'mun to translate Greek books into Arabic.[20] At any rate, none of these references relate to their appointments as head of Bayt al-Hikma.

All these fictitious elements that were added to the image of the House of Wisdom started with Brockelmann, continued with Meyerhof and Totah, and then were combined in Phillip Hitti's account of the golden age of al-Ma'mun in his popular book *History of the Arabs*, first published in 1937. The book that presented this image to a wider readership with its numerous editions and translations into Arabic and other languages, drew the standard picture of the Abbasid House of Wisdom. The most interesting element in Hitti's presentation was his assumption that the establishment of Bayt al-Hikma was the result of a determined policy.

> In pursuance of his policy, al-Ma'mun in 830 established his famous Bait al-Hikma in Baghdad, a combination of library, academy and translation bureau which in many respects proved to be the most important educational institution since the foundation of the Alexandria Museum in the first half of the third century B.C.[21]

Hitti did not elaborate on what he meant by referring to the Alexandria Museum and did not give any evidence for his claim that Bayt al-Hikma was an educational institution. In a clear-cut statement, Hitti claimed that the translation movement under al-Ma'mun and his successors centered mainly in "the newly founded academy".

To complete the image of a modern European academy, Hitti annexed the second of the two observatories founded by al-Ma'mun to this great academy.

> In connection with his Bait al-Hikma, al-Ma'mun erected at Baghdad a new shamsiyah gate, an astronomical observatory under the directorship of Sind ibn 'Ali, a converted Jew, and Yahya ibn abi-Mansur. To this observatory al-Ma'mun soon added another one on Mt. Qaysun outside Damascus.[22]

This undocumented, unauthentic image of Bayt al-Hikma was widely disseminated by the several editions of Hitti's book since 1937 until the present day,[23] as well as its concise Arabic translation (first edition 1946),[24] and drew the standard picture of Bayt al-Hikma.

In 1967, Yusuf Eche published his doctoral thesis entitled *Les Bibliotheque Arabes,* presenting the first detailed study on the House of Wisdom. This comprehensive research that he had started in 1934 on the history of what he calls public and semi-public libraries, is composed of three parts, the first of which is devoted to the Abbasid House of Wisdom and the history of the early libraries in Islam. Eche who remarkably exhausted almost all available primary sources in both published and manuscript form, does not leave much room for those who wish to search for further information about the House of Wisdom in classical literature. However, as he identifies the already established image of the House of Wisdom, he mixes the solid evidence he found with what he calls "suggestive facts/faits suggestive". For instance, he discusses the function of what the primary sources present as the "secretary of translations" (Amin ala al-Tarjama). First, he presents a hypothetical description of the duties of the holder of this position and presumes that it consists of: (1) studying the books which were acquired and choosing those that will be translated; (2) distributing the books to the translators for translation; (3) checking over the works of these translators and coordinating their work when needed; (4) after the translations were finished, presenting them to Bayt al-Hikma, where they would be copied by calligraphers and permanently recorded.[25] After a long discussion of the existing historical accounts, he arrives at the following conclusion without any proof: the translation activity centered on Bayt al-Hikma was organized according to a systematic plan. The "secretary of translations" was the highest supervisor; the work was distributed among senior translators assisted by writers, who most probably prepared the first draft; an editor was assigned to make corrections on their language. Isn't this type of an organization the most suitable one that enables it to perform its work in the most meticulous and fastest way?[26] Eche's long work dedicated to the study of the House of Wisdom and its epoch ends with the following definition of this "semi-public institute".

> It seems to us as we have shown, with sufficient reports and facts, that *Bayt al-Hikma* was established according to the Arabs' conception of this type of ancient institutions. Its founders and patrons took care to collect the works of ancient scholars, have them translated, commented on and summarized; they engaged astrologers who were equipped with instruments and probably worked in observatories and brought together scholars and staff

to deliberate and study these books and engage in debates. The caliph provided lodgings for those that worked here. We believe that we can now define the *Bayt al-Hikma* in its developed form as a quasi-public institution comprising a set of branches with the aim of developing scientific activities, such as collecting and translating books for studies and scientific productions; maintaining a staff of astrologers capable of fulfilling the patrons' wish to be foretold of the future; housing a certain number of scholars who would work there and hold what he calls "réunions spéculatives".[27]

The concoction of the House of Wisdom's false image reached its peak with a book of more than 500 pages devoted totally to its history. The author of the book claims that it was a doctoral dissertation without clearly mentioning where he defended the compilation and array of his gross errors, which unfortunately escaped the attention of academic critics. The book presents detailed information on various activities of this academy, public library, translation center, and the first Islamic university. It includes curricula of the different departments of the university (mathematical and natural sciences) furnished in an elaborate style; the payroll of the faculty members and the stipends for the students and their dormitories are also presented. Lists of the books translated from different languages are listed and the commencement ceremonies are also discussed in detail with reference to the academic dress to be worn by the teaching staff and students. The innocent ninth-century palace library of the Abbasid Caliph acquired this final image at the end of the twentieth century.[28]

It seems that the publication of Khedr Ahmed Attallah's book has encouraged scholars to publish independent monographs and "studies" on the same subject. In 1996, a master's dissertation of 252 pages titled "Beyt-ül Hikme" by Mustafa Demirci was published in Istanbul.[29] Examining this book, it is obvious that it was following the footsteps of Attallah and mainly recycling the wrong information popularized in the secondary literature.

A new episode in the long history of creating the myth was the establishment of a new national institution with the same name of the House of Wisdom in 1995 in Baghdad under the patronage of the President of the Republic. After the establishment of the new national cultural institution carrying the same name of Bayt al-Hikma in Baghdad in 1995, two publications by this institution on the Abbasid House of Sciences came through. The first, printed in 2000, was a bilingual book in Arabic and English prepared by Sundus Abbas, whose title in English reads "*Bayt'ol-Hikma constant Contribution 1200 years*". This title means that the House of Wisdom continued in its activities from the reign of Harun al-Rashid (r. 768–809) to the time of President Saddam Husain.

The second official publication by this institution was by Prof. Dr. Abd al-Jabbar Naji (2008). It was a serious academic study addressing many related questions on the history of the Abbasid House of Science. Though it relied on primary sources, however, it was still full of the exaggerated fancy depictions. For instance, Prof. Jabbar has "developed" the so-called center of translation to consist of different departments assigned to specific sorts of books on astronomy, medicine and the certain languages like "Nabataean" and "Indian" languages.

The highlight in the new episode was the organization of an international conference on the 1200th anniversary of the establishment of the Abbasid Bayt al-Hikma organized in Bagdad in 2001. The speeches and papers presented at the symposium once again registered the invented story and image of Bayt al-Hikma with additional undocumented wild exaggerations to the extent of claiming that Bayt al-Hikma had "*roots that go deep in history; that is to say in the heritage of ancient Iraq from the days of the Sumerians, the Babylonians and the Assyrians*".[30] They gave it an age that ran for "*six centuries from the third century of Hijra to mid-seventh century of Hijra*"[31] (!!) until it was burnt by Hulagu on 17 January 1258, who killed its scholars and flung the contents of its library into the waters of the Tigris".[32]

It is worth noting that the representative of the UNESCO Director-General, at the inauguration of this symposium in his tribute to the Abbasid Institution, generously identified it with UNESCO by taking the liberty of saying "accordingly I would say UNESCO would have been established here in Baghdad in the ninth century". It is also worth mentioning that the papers submitted to this "international ceremonial meeting" was published the same year in two big volumes (Volume I: 659 pages; Volume II: 556 pages).

The last study on this topic is devoted to illustrating "the ascendance of the Islamic tradition of science institutionalization" and the

> founding and patronage of academies, the example of Baghdad's Bayt al-Hikma (House of Wisdom) which flourished in the ninth century AD [which is] examined closely in the light of primary Arabic sources on the subject as well as recent contemporary international literature.

The study then goes beyond "the existing narratives on Bayt al-Hikma to argue that it was an 'academy of sciences' that preceded by centuries the *Academia dei Lincei* of Rome, considered by many scholars as the world's first academy of sciences established in 1603".[33]

With this quotation, the process of creating a myth arrives at its last destination and links the Abbasid Caliph Harun al-Rashid and Founder of the House of Wisdom Academy with the founder of the oldest Italian academy, the Italian aristocrat Federico Cesi (1585–1630), and makes the Abbasid "academy" of the ninth century a source of inspiration for the seventeenth century's first academy in Europe.

With the increasing interest among Western readers in the scientific activities within Islam, the House of Wisdom came to the fore and attracted the attention of wide segments of readership to the effect that two books in English carrying the same title of the House of Wisdom were published in 2009 and 2010.

The first book, by Jonathan Lyons, was subtitled "How the Arabs Transformed Western Civilization" and the second by Jim al-Khalili bore the subtitle "How Arabic Science Served Ancient Knowledge and Gave Us the Renaissance".

These two books are well researched and eloquently written, presenting to the western readership an attractive narrative of the scientific advancement that happened during the history of Islam and the role of these achievements in building universal advancement in science and culture. They draw on a wealth of information published for narrow circles of scholars that were not accessible to the public. However, both authors were clearly influenced by the already extant myth. For instance, J. Lyons is very convinced by the myth, stating that "al-Mansur established a royal library modelled after those of the great Persian Kings". He maintains that

> over time, the House of Wisdom came to comprise a translation bureau, a library and book repository and an academy of scholars and intellectuals from across the empire. Its overriding function, however, was the safeguarding of invaluable knowledge, a fact reflected in other terms applied at times by Arab historians to describe the project, such as the Treasury of the Books of Wisdom and simply the Treasury of Wisdom. Experts affiliated with this imperial institution staffed the caliph's observatory as well and took part in scientific experiments at his behest. But the House of Wisdom also played an important role in the cultivation of Abbasid literary works.[34]

Creating a Myth 23

Meanwhile, Prof. Jim al-Khalili, in his lively, engaging and fascinating book, mentions that "far more likely in my view is that the library, or repository of books (Khizanat), that was set up by the early caliphs was indeed distinct from al-Ma'mun academy and that the medieval Arabic historians know this".[35]

So, it is amazing that the mythical image of the House of Wisdom developed over the years and through generations of scholars and writers, became well established to the extent that the bare reality stands as an unwelcomed stranger and the myth as a household acquittance.

Notes

1 Katib Jelebi, a Mustafa ben Abdallah, *Lexicon bibliographicum et encyclopædicum: ad codicum Vindobonensium Parisiensium et Berolinensis*, edited by Gustavus Fluegel, Tomus septimus, London, 1858, 711.
2 Ibn al-Nadim, *Kitab al-fihrist*, edited by Gustav Flügel, Vol. 2, Leipzig, F.C.W. Vogel, 1871, p. 108.
3 Heinrich Suter, *Die Mathematiker und ihre werke, Abhandle zur Geschichte den Wisseneschaften Heft*.
4 Moritz Steinschneider, "Die arabischen Uebersetzungen aus dem Griechischen", *Zeitschrift der Deutschen Morgenländischen Gesellschaft*, Vol. 50, 1896, p. 201.
5 Ferdinand Wüstenfeld, *Die Academien Der Araber und Ihre Lehrer*, Göttingen, 1837.
6 Carl Brockelmann, *Geschichte der arabischen Literatur*, Vol. I, Weimar, Emil Felber Verlag, 1898, p. 202.
7 Carl Brockelmann, *Geschichte der arabischen Litteratur*, Vol. I, Leiden, E.J. Brill, 1937, pp. 220–221.
8 Carl Brockelmann, "Der Islam von seinen Anfängen bis auf die Gegenwart", in *Ullsteins Weltgeschichte. Die Entwicklung der Menschheit in Staat und Gessellschaft, in Kultur und Geistesleben vol. III: Geschichte des Orients*, edited by Pflugk-Harttung, Julius von, published by Berlin, Ullstein Verlag, 1910, p. 114; Carl Brockelmann, *Geschichte der Islamischen Völker und Staaten,* Institut für Geschischte und Kultur des Nahen Orients an der Universitat München, Verlag von R. Oldenbourg, München, 1939, pp. 114–115.
9 James E. McClellan III, *Science Reorganized*, Columbia University Press, 1983, pp. 68–74
10 Khalil Totah, *The Contribution of the Arabs to Education,* New York, Teachers College, Columbia University, 1926, pp. 26–29.
11 Khalil Totah, *Al-Tarbiya Ťnd Al-Arab*, Jerusalem 1933. Totah in the Arabic version places Bayt al-Hikma as an institution of high learning after the completion of primary and secondary education!
12 Khalid Totah, *The Contribution*, p. 28.
13 Ahmad Ferid Rifa'i, *'Asr al-Ma'mun*, Cairo, 1928.
14 Ibid., Vol. 1, pp. 373, 394.
15 The book of the *Ten Treatises on the Eye* ascribed to Huain Ibn Ishaq, translated by Max Meyerhof, Cairo, Government Press, 1928, p. XIX.

16 Ibid., p. XXII.
17 Max Meyerhof, von Alexandrien nach Bagdad, pp. 16–17.
18 Ibn Juljul, p. 65; al-Qifti, pp. 380–391; Ibn Abi Usaybia, *Uyun al-enba' fi tabaqat al- atibba'*, edited by Nizar Rıza, Beirut, Mektebet al-Hayat, p. 246.
19 Ibn Juljul, p. 69; al-Qifti, pp. 171–177; Ibn Abi Usaybia, 246.
20 Ibn Abi Usaybia, p. 260.
21 P. Hitti, *History of Arabs*, London, MacMillan, 1937, p. 310. Also see similar statement on page 410.
22 Ibid., pp. 373–375.
23 P. Hitti's book 9th edition 1968, 10th edition 1970 and reprinted many times until 2002.
24 P. Hitti, *al-Arab*, Beirut, 1946, pp. 118–119.
25 Youssef Eche, *Les bibliothèques arabes publiques et semi-publiques en Mésopotamie, en Syrie et en Égypte au Moyen Age*, Damascus, Institute Français de Damas, 1967, pp. 23–24.
26 Ibid., p. 34.
27 Ibid., p. 56.
28 Khedr Ahmed Attallah, *Bayt al-Hikma fi 'Asr al-'Abbasyyin*, Cairo, Dar Al Fikr Al-Araby, n.d.
29 Mustafa Demirci, *Beytü'l-Hikme*, İnsan Yayınları, 2016.
30 See (the Book of collection of Papers delivered on the 1200th Anniversary of the Foundation of Bayt al-Hikma) Bayt al-Hikma al-Abbasi: A'rakat al-Madi ve Ru'yat al-Hadır, Baghdad, Bayt al-Hikma Institution Publishing, 2001, p. 21.
31 Ibid., p. 3.
32 Ibid., p. 13.
33 Moneed Rafe' Zou'bi, Mohd Hazim Shah, *Science Institutionalization in Early Islam*, DAR Publisher, The University of Jordan, 2015.
34 Jonathan Lyons, *The House of Wisdom*, Newark, P. Bloomsbury Press, 2009, p. 63.
35 Jim Al-Khalili, *The House of Wisdom*, London, Penguin Books, 2010, p. 70.

Part III Dissecting the Myth

Careful and critical examination of the available information provided by the few primary sources that have reached us will undoubtedly clarify many misunderstandings and help to undo the fanciful portrait of the Bayt al-Hikma's myth as a modern academy. Certain bibliographical and biographical dictionaries written between the tenth to thirteenth centuries have references to the scholarly activities in the early Abbasid period where some belong to the royal library at the Abbasid court in Baghdad. These books provide many examples of caliphal patronage and support to scholars whether or not they were associated with this library during the time of Harun al-Rashid and al-Mamun, and they give clues to the nature of this library.

At the forefront of these references is the *Fihrist* of al-Nadim (d. 990), the Baghdadi bibliophile, bibliographer, and copyist of manuscripts who compiled the most detailed information on the literary activities and the cultural legacy of the first centuries of Islamic history, and produced his monumental work widely known as *al-Fihrist* (meaning, the book catalogue) whose draft was completed in 988, almost 200 years after the creation of the said Library.

Among the other sources, we can point to Tabaqat books, that is, biographical dictionaries of al-Nadim's contemporary, the Andalusian physician Ibn Juhul (d. 994), the Egyptian Ibn al-Qifti (d. 1248), and the Damascene Ibn Abi Usaybia (d. 1270). In addition, the Syriac historian and theologian Ibn al-Ibri, also known as Bar Hebraeus (d. 1286) in his book *Tarih Mukhtasar al-Duwal*, sheds light on some cases. These sources occasionally offer some more information. Other than these, the later sources do not provide much that is not already known. It is worth mentioning here that these sources were written between 200 and 400 years after the appearance of the Bayt al-Hikma. Al-Nadim's *Fihrist* undoubtedly is the most important source because of the short time interval and the fact that he lived in Bagdad and was

DOI: 10.4324/9781003323679-3

well connected with scholars, book lovers, and book traders thanks to the business he inherited from his father.

In the *Fihrist*, there are few clear references to Bayt al-Hikma and its alternative appellations as Khizanat al-Hikme and others. The *Fihrist* specifies certain names and certain persons who were associated with Bayt al-Hikma with their occupation. First among these is the name of Sâlm who is identified as the *Sahib* of Bayt al-Hikma.[1] The word *sahib* could be rendered as head, responsible figure, or director. The second one to be qualified as the Sahib/head of Bayt al-Hikma is *Sahl Ibn Harun*[2] during the reign of al-Ma'mun. In different contexts, al-Nadim mentions that *Sahl Ibn Harun* was in the service of al-Ma'mun and that he was in charge (*sahib*) of the royal library but here he uses different appellation instead of Bayt al-Hikma, he uses Khizanat al-Hikma.[3] Al-Nadim also mentions a position of a *Sharik*, meaning an associate/companion of the head of Bayt al-Hikma and notes the name of Said Ibn Huraym al-Katib as Sharik of Sahl Ibn Harun in Bayt al-Hikma.[4]

Among others who held a specific occupation, Allan al-Shu'ubi[5] is mentioned by al-Nadim as a copyist who produces copies of books for Harun al-Rashid, al-Ma'mun, and the Barmakides. He also mentions ten names of bookbinders and the first he provides is Ibn Ali Al-Haryish.[6] He says "he was book binding at the khizanat al-Hikma of al-Ma'mun".

The primary sources other than *al-Fihrist* referred to above add little to what al-Nadim provided in his *Fihrist*; however, occasionally some supplementary information was added to clarify certain ambiguities. For instance, al-Nadim in his account on al-Fadl Abu Sahl bin Newabakht mentions that he was working in the Repository of Wisdom (Khizanat al-Hikma) for Harun al-Rashid and he would translate Persian books for him. Al-Qifti in his biographical dictionary added that Harun al-Rashid appointed him to be in charge of the "Repository of Books on Wisdom".

If we scrutinize the array of information and references in the *Fihrist*, though few, we come to clear examples about the personal involvement of the caliphs and their Viziers with the scholarly activities of Bayt al-Hikma.

Al-Nadim narrates that Harun al-Rashid's vizier Yahya Khalid bin Barmak was the first person to become interested in Almagest and he asked Abu Hassan and Sâlm to revise and edit a translation of Ptolemy's Almagest that he was not pleased with, so they brought the experienced translators and both of them examined their work and approved the clearest and most eloquent of their translations.[7]

Dissecting the Myth 27

This short account gives clear insight into how the Bayt al-Hikma worked and what its head functions were. Meanwhile, it shows also that Bayt al-Hikma's services were not limited to the caliph.

One of the rare accounts that enlightens the role of the Bayt al-Hikma in scholarly activities is what al-Nadim tells us about the famous mathematician, astronomer, and polymath Mohammed bin Musa al-Khwarizmi's (d. 850) association with Khizanat al-Hikma.[8] He says that al-Khwarizmi was solely devoted to Bayt al-Hikma (Munaqati) during al-Ma'mun's time.[9] This account shows that there were different degrees of the association of scholars with Bayt al-Hikma.

Al-Nadim in different places of his *Fihrist* gives information about his personal experiences with books related to or supposedly belonging to the library of al-Ma'mun. In the first section of the first chapter, where he writes about the languages of Arabs and foreign people, he makes two clear references to the library of al-Ma'mun. In the first example, he says

> I myself have seen a passage in the library of Al-Ma'mun which I have translated of what the commander of the faithful Abd'Allah al-Ma'mun, may Allah honor him, ordered the translators to transcribe. It contained Himyarite script, and I give you an exact reproduction of what was in the transcription ...[10]

In the second example, he says

> the Abyssinians have a script like the Himyarite letters going from left to right. They separated each of the words by means of three dots, dotted like triangle between the letter of two words. This is an example of the letters which I copied from the library of Al-Ma'mun ...[11]

After these clear indications of al-Nadim's visits to the library of al-Ma'mun and his personal examination of the books, he gives us different examples of his precarious experiences. In the same first section of the First Chapter of the *Fihrist*, he says "there was in the library of al-Ma'mun, something written on hide, in the handwriting of Abd al-Muttalib Ibn Hisham [the grandfather of prophet Mohamad] mentioning the claim of Abd al-Muttalib ibn Hisham of Mecca against so-and-so ...".[12] In the second section of First Chapter of his *Fihrist*, al-Nadim says "I once read a book which fell in my hands, and which was an ancient transcription, apparently from the library

28 *Dissecting the Myth*

of al-Ma'mun. In it the copyist mentions the names and numbers of scripture and revealed books ...".[13]

It is obvious from the above mentioned four accounts about the personal experiences of al-Nadim with the books belonging to the library of al-Ma'mun that there were books that he saw and took notes inside the library and other ones outside the library where he says "fell in my hands" or "was in the library of al-Ma'mun". These expressions, when also considered with the statement of Ibn Abi Usaybia that he saw books carrying the sign of al-Ma'mun [library] (see Part VIII), suggest that 400 years after the death of al-Ma'mun, books belonging to his library were changing hands.

A Bayt al-Hikma and Translation Movement

Regarding Bayt al-Hikma's role in the translation movement that occurred in the Abbasid period, there is a discrepancy between the historical reality as described by the primary sources and the maximalist image portraited by Meyerhof[14] and Fück[15] who maintained that there was a "translation bureau" where translation from different languages were made, whereas modern historians such as Ira Lapidus further argue that it was a translation school.[16]

Al-Nadim is silent on this aspect of translation activities but his contemporary, the Andalusian physician Ibn Juljul (944–994) in his dictionary of biographies of physicians and philosophers, mentions three important names (Yuhanna Ibn Masawayh, Yuhanna bin al-Batriq, and Hunayn Ibn Ishaq) who supervised and were entrusted to the translation activities under different Abbasid Caliphs.[17] We understand from Ibn Juljul's accounts that those translations were made under the authority of somebody called *Amin ala al-Tarjama* (superintendent/secretary of translation) who was to supervise the translations.

In writing the biography of Hunayn Ibn Ishaq, a Nestorian Christian Arab from Hira, Ibn Juljul says that Hunayn Ibn Ishaq studied medicine with Yuhanna Ibn Masawayh in Baghdad; he was probably bilingual in Syriac and Arabic and perfected his Greek. He also tells us that Hunayn was assigned the duties of *Amin* of translation by al-Mutawakkil (r. 847–861) and he was put in charge of conducting translation activities. He was also assigned the best translators and scribes of the time. He himself translated the medical texts of Hippocrates and Galen from Greek into Arabic and wrote some works that were based on Greek sources. Hunayn's perfection in languages is also praised in his biography.[18]

Dissecting the Myth 29

In order to clarify the information in the available historical accounts as much as possible, whether the translation was an institutional or rather, an individual process, a careful study of the list of works of Hunayn Ibn Ishaq should shed light on this issue.[19] This has been a controversial issue since the famous study of Max Meyerhof published in 1928, which we referred to previously.

The valuable information found in the long bibliographic list of the translations of Galen's works made by Hunayn Ibn Ishaq and recorded in his epistle to Ali bin Yahya gives significant clues as to how, why, and for whom this important chapter of the translation movement was carried out. The translation activities that he made individually or together with his colleagues and students lasted more than 30 years. Among the frequently mentioned names that placed orders for numerous translations during his productive years are physicians, the Banu Musa brothers, famous intellectual statesmen of the period, and private library owners.[20]

In listing his numerous translations, Hunayn only notes that some of them were made during the periods of Caliphs al-Ma'mun, al-Mutawakkil, and al-Wathiq (r. 842–847) but does not mention in any case that these translations were ordered by them; for instance, he mentions that he translated certain works to Yahya bin Musawayh during the reign of al-Mutawakkil and to Muhammed bin Musa during the reign of al-Wathiq. We note that the names and identities of the people that placed the orders differ according to their preferred language. If the translation is from Greek to Syriac, it is obvious that the people that placed the orders are the physicians that came from Jundishapur to Baghdad. If the translated works are in Arabic, it is possible to find people of Arabic origin or Arabic-speaking people among those who have placed the orders.

Among the many works personally translated, revised, or edited by Hunayn, there is no information indicating that they were made in the name of the House of Wisdom or any other institution. Yuhanna Ibn Masawayh (d. 243/857),[21] who was Hunayn's teacher, was among the names listed; considering that he was a physician and the founder of the Bimaristan in Baghdad and had need for the translations of Galen's works in this capacity, it is obvious that the translations made by Hunayn from Greek into Syriac were for the benefit of Masawayh as well as the other physicians that came from Jundishapur. Probably, here we can trace an institutional dimension through the Bimaristan in creating the demand for translation of medical texts.

In fact, it is clear that these translations were made upon professional request and did not have any connection with the House of

Wisdom. The orders placed for other translations indicate that they were made for scholars, interested statesmen, and private library owners. Considering that the Banu Musa, according to al-Nadim[22] paid approximately 500 dinars a month to several translators including Hunayn, Thabit Ibn Qurra, and others for their services in compiling, translating books, and attendance (mulazama) means that the translation movement at this time was not a monopoly belonging to the caliph and was not limited to the House of Wisdom.

Regarding the places where these translations were made, it did not have to be in a specific place; as with other compilations and writings, it could be anywhere that provided the facility for intellectual work. There is an interesting anecdote among the information given by Hunayn. While working with Salmawayh in correcting the Syriac translation of one of Galen's works that was badly translated, Hunayn had the Greek text and Salmawayh had the Syriac translation; they compared the two and started to make the corrections according to the original text. Meanwhile, he emphasizes that correcting a bad translation was more difficult than translating the original text; he adds that Salmawayh told him better to translate this work from its Greek original. In giving this explanation, he states that he completed the translation during al-Ma'mun's military campaign to al-Raqqa; that is, while they were accompanying the army. In addition to these interesting remarks, he says that after completing it, the translation was sent to Baghdad for copying but unfortunately the book was burnt due to the fire erupted in the ship.[23]

In evaluating the examples and information included in his long bibliography, the main conclusion to be drawn is that there was no "center" or "bureau" of translation as a distinct department of the House of Wisdom which Meyerhof claimed. There is no indication that Hunayn was given an official title or position to administrate and supervise the whole translations. There is also no reference that the title of *Amin ala al-Tarjama* put forward by Ibn Juljul. More importantly, not all translations made in the early Abbasid period were conducted in the House of Wisdom under royal patronage. There is no supporting information or evidence for this claim. Ibn Juljul's reference to Hunayn was to the effect that he was entrusted with translations, made translations himself, and helped to supervise and edit the translations made by others. It is obvious that the development of the translation movement, like other literature, compilation, and other creative intellectual pursuits were enhanced by the patronage and encouragement of not only the caliphs but also the individuals, as well as the emergence of demanding readership among the courtly elites and intellectuals, as well as interested professionals of his time. At any rate, the nonexistence of specific information about the role of the House of Wisdom in the translation movement should not mean that the House of Wisdom did not witness scholars and translators who were engaged in translating texts and contributing to the translation movement.

B Bayt al-Hikma as a University

One of the farfetched assumptions in some modern writings on the Bayt al-Hikma is that it was not only a university[24] but also the first Islamic University where medicine was taught[25] and had its own endowment.[26] A few lines in two primary sources about a specific case of education or the training of three brilliant orphans unbelievably transformed Bayt al-Hikma into a full-fledged modern university with detailed information about education levels, contents, payrolls of its faculty members, and details on academic ceremonies and regalia.[27]

Al-Qifti in reporting on the death of Musa bin Shakir, one of al-Ma'mun's astronomers, mentions that the caliph took special interest in his three genius sons Muhammed, Ahmad, and Hasan also known as the Banu Musa al-Munajjim (sons of Musa the astronomer) and closely supervised their education and the way they were brought up. Yahya bin Mansur, one of al-Ma'mun's prominent astronomers, was ordered to take them under his care. Soon they excelled in mathematics, astronomy, geometry, and mechanics. The words of al-Qifti on this occasion related to Bayt al-Hikma reads as: "... al-Ma'mun put Ishaq Ibn Ibrahim al-Mouslabi in charge of the three young boys and he placed them (*athbetahum*) with Yahya bin Abi Mansur at Bayt al-Hikma.[28] This piece of information which is repeated by Ibn al-Ibri[29] in a shorter version does not allow us to draw an explicit conclusion. It only reflects al-Ma'mun's patronage of the three young sons of Musa out of respect for the memory of their father as well as his appreciation of their talents. It also seems to imply that indeed some teaching took place in Bayt al-Hikma but not in an institutionalized form. Rather the teaching of the Banu Musa seems to have been patterned according to the personalized traditional system of transmission from master to disciple. Furthermore, nowhere else can one find similar statements confirming the possibility of regular, organized teaching in Bayt al-Hikma, let alone a full-fledged modern university.

It is amazing to see how al-Qifti and Ibn al-Ibri's short, clear, and concise statements were amplified in fancy details without any support of historical evidence. Attallah claims that the education in the Bayt al-Hikma was divided into three stages. The first stage goes from the age of 6 to the age of 14 years and happens outside the institution by learning the Qur'an, writing, reading, grammar, and arithmetic. In the second stage from 14 to 18 the student stays in this surroundings and studies some of the religious sciences like Fıqh and Tafsir with an understanding of the Qur'an. The last stage of Attallah's concept of study in the Bayt al-Hikma is finally the study in the institution itself, but in two different systems. The first is the system of lectures, the second is the system of conversation and discussion. The student will be taught in the philosophical and the medical sciences, astronomy, natural sciences, geography, and music. Attallah even explains how the teacher organize their classes.[30] But this explanation for the work inside the Bayt al-Hikma appears more like a fanciful tale than a description of an Abbasid era institution.

Another point of confusion in the constructed modern image of Bayt al-Hikma is its relation with the two observatories built by al-Ma'mun.[31] This is despite the clarifications made by Aydın Sayılı in his book *The Observatory in Islam* (1960) that the activities of these two institutions, meaning the observatory and Bayt al-Hikma, were sufficiently distinct in nature and the overlapping of personalities with them were slight, if any.[32] Sayılı underlines the fact that these first observatories in Islam were independent institutions which were not a part of the Bayt al-Hikma. However, it is still astonishing to read about the supposed great complex of scientific institutions of Bayt al-Hikma.

Notes

1 AN I, p. 374; AN II, pp. 142, 215, 326.
2 AN I, p. 25.
3 AN I, p. 373.
4 AN I, p. 373.
5 AN I, p. 326.
6 AN I, p. 24.
7 AN II, p. 215.
8 Rosenfeld-Ihsanoglu, No. 41.
9 AN II, p. 235.
10 AN I, p. 14; Dodge, pp. 9–10.
11 AN I, p. 44, Dodge, p. 36.
12 AN I, p. 13; Dodge, p. 9.
13 AN I, p. 51; Dodge, p. 41.
14 Max Meyerhof, 1930, p. 16 (402).

Dissecting the Myth 33

15 Johann Fück, *Arabische Kultur und Islam im Mittelalter: ausgewahlte Schriften*, edited by Manfred Fleischhammer, Wiemar, Hermann Böhlaus Nachfolger, 1981, p. 306.
16 Ira M. Lapidus, 1988, p. 94.
17 Ibn Juljul, pp. 65, 67, 68, 89.
18 Ibn Juljul, pp. 68, 69.
19 On Hunayn and his works see Rosenfeld-İhsanoğlu, 37
20 Hunayn ibn Ishaq, Über Die Syrischen und Arabischen Galenübersetzungen, zum Ersten Mal Herausgegeben und uberstat von G. Bergstrasser, Leipzig, 1925, p. 241. For reprint of this long list, see Fuat Sezgin, *Arab-Islamic History of Science*, Islamic Medicine, Vol. 18, published by the Institute of History of Arabic-Islamic Science, Frankfurt, 2008.
21 For Masawayh, see Rosenfeld, İhsanoğlu, p. 32.
22 AN. II, p. 143.
23 Hunayn ibn Ishaq, Über Die Syrischen..., p. 224.
24 H.U. Rahman, *A Chronology of Islamic History, 570–1000 CE*, London, Ta-Ha Publishers, 1994, p. 179.
25 Khedr Ahmed Attallah, p. 244.
26 Ibid., 99.
27 Ibid., pp. 140, 141.
28 Al-Qifti, pp. 441, 442. AN. II, pp. 224–226; Rosenfeld-Ihsanoglu, no: 72.
29 Ibn al-Ibri, 1890, p. 364.
30 Khedr Ahmed Attallah, pp. 140, 141.
31 Youssef Eche, 1967, p. 56; Ira M. Lapidus, 1988, p. 94; D. Sourdel, "Bayt al-Hikma", *Encyclopedia of Islam*, 2nd Edition, 1960, p. 1141.
32 Aydın Sayılı, *Observatory in Islam and Its Place in the General History of the Observatory*, Ankara, Türk Tarih Kurumu, 1988, pp. 50, 56. Sayılı's book's first edition was published in 1960.

Part IV What to Call a Library in Arabic?

One of the main reasons for the confusion related to the nature of the court library, called Bayt al-Hikma, was due to its name, which had no precedence in the classic Arabic language. To clarify the misunderstandings about this institution which was called by different names in different contexts, it is essential to examine the development of the Arabic term or terms for "library" which were not known by the Arabs in their pre-Islamic life; then we can determine how the compound name of "Bayt al-Hikma" developed.

The question here is to find out how the Arabic wording for a library came about. The information at hand shows that there was no specific term for such an institution in pre-Islamic Arabic languages. The first examples for book collections or what would be "libraries" in the early centuries of Islam are reported by different appellations; there was no standard terminology.[1]

One of the first references to a place where books were kept was made by al-Balazuri (d. 279/892) in his report on the assassination of the third Caliph Osman (d. 35/636). He narrated that Marwan Ibn al-Hakam's (d. 685) nursemaid Fatma bint Sharik al-Ansariyya had ordered that Marwan, who had received a blow on the head during the assault, be carried into the "house *(bayt)* where the books were placed".[2] A second reference relates to the collection of books that belonged to Mohammed bin Jubayr bin Mut'am (died before 99/718), who was the son of one of the Prophet's companions and a narrator of Quraishi traditions. Ibn 'Asakir (d. 571/1175) reports that Mohammed bin Jubayr bin Mut'am kept books in a locked *bayt* and the key was in the safekeeping of his slave girl. He had ordered her: "When someone requests anything from this house give him the key but do not lose any of the books".[3] In the years heralding the end of the first Hijra century, there were places in Mecca where books were kept and where friends and acquaintances socialized. Abu al-Faraj al-Isfahani (d. 967) and

DOI: 10.4324/9781003323679-4

What to Call a Library in Arabic? 35

Ibn Hazım al-Andalusi (d. 1064) relate that Abd al-Hakem Ibn Amr bin Abid Allah Ibn Safwan al-Jamhî's house near the holy Ka'ba was the place where his friends met and played chess and backgammon, while others spent their time reading the books on various sciences placed here for their pleasure and the children played a game called "qirqat". In two sources, the word used for this house that resembled a private club was *bayt*.[4]

As seen from the above examples, the historical narratives are not explicit about the existence of libraries in the conventional sense but rather about the existence of collections of some books and notebooks kept in certain places called *bayt* (house), without using a special term for a library. However, there is a surviving account about Caliph Mu'awiyya (r. 41–60/661–680) that was recorded in the third/ninth century where the appellation Bayt al-Hikma is mentioned. This account is about a debate between Osman bin Said al-Darimi (815–893) and Bishr al-Marisi (d. 833) where it is reported that there was a place called "Bayt al-Hikma" where Mu'awiyya kept the written texts of hadiths belonging to Prophet Muhammad.[5] A century later, when giving an account of Mu'awiyya's daily life, al-Masudi (d. 345/956) talks about the existence of a library without an explicit appellation. This was where Mu'awiyya had kept the *defatir* (notebooks) containing histories and biographies of the past kings, which were read to him at night.[6] The usage of Bayt al-Hikma in the above-mentioned text does not necessarily mean that this term was used in Muawiya's time as Eche suggested.[7] Notwithstanding the authenticity of the author's account, this appellation attributed by Bishr al-Marisi, who died during the reign of al-Ma'mun, corresponds to the time when the compound name Bayt al-Hikma was used as a term denoting the prestigious caliphal library that had a prominent place in the cultural life of Baghdad. It is obvious that this appellation was already established and commonly used during the Abbasid period. One of the early accounts which refers to the existence of libraries in the Umayyad epoch is mentioned by Ibn Juljul. In his account of the translations made by Masarjawaih during the reign of the Umayyad Caliph Marwan I (r. 684–5), he uses the appellation *Khazain al-Kutub* (repositories of books).[8]

The socio-economic development and the emergence of urban society in Baghdad in the early Abbasid period gave rise to a growing interest in learning. As explained in the introductory remarks on Baghdad and the rise of interest in the foreign sciences, the cosmopolitan elite's interest in pursuing and patronizing the cultural activities and emulating their caliphs led to the emergence of both private book collections and libraries due to the availability and accessibility of paper as a cheap writing material. Hence the words *khizane, repository* and *Bayt* (house) that denoted a place for keeping and safeguarding these books made their appearance in the literature that described this period.[9] Sources usually use the word khizana for the libraries owned by scholars and bibliophiles associated with the Abbasid Caliphs. Here the words "khizana" and "bayt" refer to the library as a building and (books) "kutub" or (wisdom) "hikma" as the contents of the library. "Khizana" comes from the root "khazana" and its literal meaning is to reposit, store, etc., hence khizana means repository, storeroom or a small chamber within a large chamber.[10] The second word "bayt" has a similar meaning though originally it signifies a tent made up of several poles that was commonly used as a house, a chamber or an apartment. At later stages in the history of the development of institutions of learning in Islam, the word *dar* would be used for bigger places than a *bayt*, comprises a court or a set of apartments.[11] The above-mentioned two words khizana and bayt were used interchangeably by al-Nadim to denote the palace library where the books (kutub) that were mainly related to wisdom (hikma) were kept. The palace library was the repository (khizana) or the house (bayt) of books of wisdom, a word, which in this context denotes that the subjects of these books were related primarily to the foreign sciences and philosophy, that is, nonreligious sciences introduced from Indian, Sassanian, Syriac, and Greek sources, which were mainly known as *hikma*.

A careful examination of al-Nadim's few references clearly shows that he refers to the palace library of the two caliphs with different combinations of the above-mentioned words. It seems that some scholars took these variants as expressions of different institutions and presumed that the compound name "Bayt al-Hikma" was the appellation for a different institution which they thought was more than a palace library.

It will be noted below that there are two ways of expressing the attributes of the word *khizana*. The first and most often used word that has become a standard term for libraries is *Khizanat al-Kutub* literally meaning Repository of Books. The second term is *Khizanat al-Hikma* and refers to certain types of books kept in the library. The following examples may be self-explanatory. Ali b. Yahya al-Munajjim (d. 275/888), who was the court companion *(nedim)* of both al-Mutawakkil and al-Mu'tamid (r. 870–892), owned a library. The extant historic accounts about this library state that, "There was a great library (Khizanat Kutub/repository of books) in his palace which he used to call Khizanat al-Hikma".[12] Al-Nadim, in referring to the library of Ali bin Ahmed al-Imrani (d. 955/956) where he saw and used its books during his visits, simply uses the term khizane. Meanwhile, as for the library that was founded by Fath Ibn Khaqan (d. 247/861), one of the closest associates of Mutawakkil, he alternatively uses Khizanat al-Hikma (I, 160; II 442)[13] or briefly Khizane (I, 130).[14]

From these examples and many more, which are in the relevant literature, it may be concluded that in the early Abbasid period and probably soon before it, the term *khizanat al-kutub* (repository of books) was established as an Arabic term for library with its short form being *khizana*. It seems that at the Western end of the Abbasid Caliphate in al-Andalus, this term and its plural form *Khazain al-Kutub* was the only term used for libraries, whether its book collection was Islamic or pre-Islamic and its status private or royal. Ibn Juljul, when referring to both Greek and Umayyad libraries, used the same appellation.[15] Obviously, the attribute *hikma/wisdom* was used to designate the nature of the books that comprised the library collection. The compound name of the *Khizanat Kutub al-Hikma* meaning the Repository of Wisdom Books was later abbreviated to Khizanat al-Hikma, that is, the repository of wisdom.[16] This then became qualified as the Bayt al-Hikma, that is to say the House of Wisdom, when it grows larger and its content were mainly composed of books of the pre-Islamic heritage (hikma) during the reign of both al-Rashid and al-Ma'mun.

It should be noted here that there is a clear resemblance between the newly coined Arabic name for library Khizanat al-Kutub and the well-established Greek word *bibliothêkê*. Both terms are compound nouns denoting books and where they are enclosed or kept. In Greek, biblio means book and thêkê means case where the books were kept.[17] So it is very obvious that the Arabic appellation for library is similar to the Greek one. However, despite such resemblance, it is not so easy to claim that the Arabic term was a translation of the Greek one in the absence of textual evidence. On the contrary it seems from Manfred Ullmann's Dictionary of ninth-century Greek-Arabic Translations that the word bibliothêkê was not among the Greek words translated to Arabic in the ninth century whereas there are certain compound nouns formed with thêkê.[18]

Notes

1 Y. Eche (pp. 63, 64) was the first to assemble and study examples. It is clear from the newer publications related to the same subject that he had almost exhausted the sources. See also Majid b. 'Abbud b. Sa'id Badahdah,

38 What to Call a Library in Arabic?

"Books and Bookmaking during the Time of Prophet Mohammed (Peace be Upon Him) and Khula fa'al al-Rashideen; Effects and Initiatives", Master's Thesis, King Abdul Aziz University, 1999, pp. 529–532.

2 Al-Balazuri, *Kitab Jumal min Ansab al-Ashraf*, edited by Suhayl Zakkar, Riyad Zirikli, Vol. 6, Beirut, Dar al-Fikr, 1996, p. 198.

3 Ibn Asakir, *Tarikh Madinat Dimashq*, Vol. 52, edited by Omar Ibn Gharamah al-'Amrawi, Beirut, Dar al-Fikr, 1997, p. 187.

4 Abu al-Faradj al-Isfahani, *Al-Aghani*, Vol. 4, Cairo, Wizarat al-Thaqafa wa al-Irshad al Qawmi, n.d., p. 253; Ibn Hazm al-Andalusi, *Djamharat Ansab al-Arab*, edited by Levi Provençal, Cairo, Dar al-Maarif, 1948, p. 150 and Abd al-Salam Mohammad Harun, 5th Edition, Cairo, Dar al-Maarif, 1982, p. 160.

5 Al-Darimi, *Rad al-Imam al-Darimi 'Osman b. Sa'id 'ala Bash al-Marisi al 'Anid*, edited by Muhammad Hamid al-Faqi, Beirut, Dar al-Kutub al-'Ilmiyya, n.d., p. 15; Y. Eche, *Les Bibliothéque Arab* 11, Fn. 2.

6 Al-Masudi, *Muruj al-Zahab*, Cairo, 1249 (2/27); Y. Eche, *Les Bibliothéque Arab*, 12, Fn. 1.

7 Y. Eche, *Les Bibliothéque Arab*, p. 11.

8 Ibn Juljul, p. 61.

9 For new survey on Umayyad and Abbasid libraries, see, İsmail E. Erünsal, *Ortaçağ İslam Dünyasında Kitap ve Kütüphane*, İstanbul, Timaş Yayınları, 2018, pp. 326–339.

10 E.W. Lane, p. 734.

11 E.W. Lane, pp. 280, 931.

12 Yaqut al-Hamawi, *Mu'jam al-Udaba*, Vol. 15, Cairo, Dar al-Ma'mun, n.d., p. 157.

13 AN, p. 160, Vol. 2, p. 442 (New Edition).

14 AN, p. 130.

15 Ibn Juljul, *Tabaqat al-'Atibba*, pp. 39, 61.

16 Al-Nadim (AN II, p. 234), calls the place where Abu Sahl al-Fadl ibn Naubakht worked *Khizanat al-Hikma*, in its abbreviated form, while Al-Qifti (p 255) writes it as *Khizanat Kutub al-Hikma*.

17 A Greek-English Lexicon, compiled by Henry George Liddel and Robert Schott, Oxford, Clarendon Press, 1968, p. 315.

18 Manfred Ullmann, *Wörterbuch Zu den Grichisch-Arabischen Übersetzungen des 9. Jahrhunderts*, Harrowitz Verlag, Wiesbaden, 2002, pp. 120, 666.

Part V What Was the Abbasid Caliph's Library Called?

The sources at hand do not have sufficient information to ascertain when the first library in the Abbasid court was established, however at the outset it is safe to say that the beginning of such a library would accompany the translation movement and scholarly activities, which started with the personal attention and interest of al-Mansur (r. 754–775), the second Abbasid Caliph and the founder of the city of Baghdad, and his circle. According to Sa'id al-Andalusi (d. 1070), al-Mansur was the first Abbasid Caliph to cultivate science and in addition to his profound knowledge of logic and jurisprudence, he was very interested in philosophy and observational astronomy and the people who worked in these fields.[1] This keen interest in science and learning no doubt acted as a kind of motive to establish a library in the palace. According to Katip Celebi (d. 1657), al-Mansur asked the Byzantine emperor to send him science books and the emperor sent him Euclid's books and others.[2] Al-Masudi (d. 956) tells us that "Once in possession of these books, the public read and studied them avidly".[3] The available information in the narratives of the early Abbasid period is explicit about the existence of the palace library during the reigns of Harun al-Rashid (r. 786–809) and his son al-Ma'mun (r. 813–833). This information is mostly found in the *al-Fihrist* of al-Nadim (d. 990), as well as in other historical accounts relating to that period. According to these sources, the presence of a library attached to or within the palace complex during the reigns of Harun al-Rashid and al-Ma'mun is a well-established fact, as will be seen in the next chapter.

Al-Nadim, in his frequent references to this library as already explained, uses different names made up of a combination of the words *Khizana* (repository), *Bayt* (house), *Kutub* (books), and *Hikma* (wisdom). It is obvious that he refers to the same library, which belongs to the same caliph, with more than one compound name composed from these words. For example, in one place he states that Sahl bin

DOI: 10.4324/9781003323679-5

Harun was in the service of al-Ma'mun as the director of Repository of Wisdom (Sahib Khizanat al-Hikma),[4] while in another place he mentions that he was the director of the House of Wisdom (Sahib Bayt al-Hikma).[5]

Al-Nadim, in his short references to Sahl bin Harun, Said bin Huraym and Salm, notes that Sahl entered the service of al-Ma'mun and became the director (sahib) of the Repository of Wisdom "Khizanat al-Hikma". Later he refers to Said bin Huraym as the partner *sharik* of Sahl bin Harun in the House of Wisdom "Bayt al-Hikma".[6] As for Salm, he says twice that Salm was the director of the House of Wisdom[7] and once said that he was the director in association *Ma'* with Sahl bin Harun.[8] All these imply that there was more than one administrator at the same time at Bayt al-Hikma. Meanwhile, he clearly mentions al-Ma'mun's library by two different names.

Although the above-mentioned two terms refer to the same institution, we understand that the compound name Bayt al-Hikma was used mainly for the caliph's library, distinguishing it from the other libraries or any repository for books. The literal meanings of the words "khizana" and "bayt" as explained above show the difference in identification and capacity.

Al-Nadim in general uses the name Khizana for the libraries of Abbasid Caliphs (e.g., Khizanat al-Mu-tadid) excepting those of Harun al-Rashid and al-Ma'mun.[9] Surprisingly he takes great care in using the different names for al-Ma'mun's library. In writing about the scholarly activities in al-Ma'mun's time, he uses the names Bayt al-Hikma[10] or Khizanat al-Hikma;[11] however, when he refers to what remained from this library in his own time, while he is listing the books that belonged to this library, he calls it Khizanat al-Ma'mun.[12]

His "selective appellation" is not an oversight or due to his usage of synonyms. It is evident from the information we have at hand that calling the palace library Bayt al-Hikma in the periods of Harun al-Rashid and al-Ma'mun was not only because they housed books related to what has been called wisdom but also due to their housing the kinds of scholarly activities related to topics in these books of wisdom. For al-Nadim, who wrote his work one and half centuries after al-Ma'mun's death, what remained of this library was no different from the other libraries that collected books including books on wisdom without being the venue for scholarly activities that distinguished the two caliphs' library from the others.

It is a well-established fact that the two caliphs, who owned this library known as Bayt al-Hikma, were after the books of the pre-Islamic cultures that were in their lands and in the neighboring countries outside their domain, specifically the books in the Byzantine collections. Considering their close interest in the history and culture of the Greeks and Persians, it is plausible that they were aware of the famous ancient libraries belonging to these two worlds. However, we do not possess information to verify whether they took the ancient libraries as models in establishing their own, as maintained by farfetched assertions that we come across in modern scholarship. There is no evidence that this term was translated from Greek or Persian, furthermore, those who maintain this viewpoint have not even provided the Greek or Persian equivalent of this compound name or even of the word "library" in those languages.

Youssef Eche, who was one of the first scholars to study the history of Bayt al-Hikma in detail, maintains that the Arabs began to build libraries similar to those found in the lands that they conquered and called them Bayt al-Hikma or Khizanat al-Hikma. Without giving any historical example or proof, he claims that this appellation is the Arabic translation of the names of pre-Islamic institutions. Eche also alludes to what he considers as similarities between the Abbasid Bayt al-Hikma and the Museum of Alexandria and draws parallels between the two. He supports his suggestion by anachronistic evidence taken from al-Biruni (d. 1050) and al-Maqrizi (d. 1442), based on their accounts of Greek and ancient Egyptian institutions.[13] The two quotations that Eche refers to as Bayt al-Hikma and Dar al-Hikma do not substantiate the claim that these were the original appellations of pre-Islamic institutions, as much as they give good examples for the common usage of this compound name as an established name for institutions dealing with sciences related to pre-Islamic civilizations.

In related Arabic literature there are many clear examples that show the term House of Wisdom after it was coined and became frequently used to denote ancient Greek institutions dealing with science and philosophy. The famous Abbasid author and translator Hunayn Ibn Ishaq (d. 873), a century before al-Nadim, in his book *Adâb al-Falâsifa* writing about the meetings of Greek philosophers, says that they met in one house of the houses of wisdom (Beyt min buyut al-Hikma) to discuss philosophy, letters, and wisdom.[14] It is clear that he is using this newly coined Arabic term as an attribution for the Greek institution where Greek philosophers would meet. In Part VI, we will elaborate on this point further.

The famous geographer Ibn Hawqal (died after 973), who lived in Baghdad, briefly mentions Rome and Athens in his work *Suret al-Ard*. He calls Athens "Dar Hikmet al-Yunaniyin"; that is, the house or seat of wisdom of the Greeks.[15] In his brief explanation, Ibn Hawqal states that "sciences and philosophy/ulum wa Hikma" of the old Greeks were preserved in Athens, which was considered to be the house of wisdom. It is interesting that Ibn Hawqal uses the word "dar", a synonym of "bayt" which specifically means a large-sized mansion, a house comprising a court or a set of apartments.[16] Contrary to Ibn Hawqal, al-Nadim in his different accounts on the Greek philosophers and Aristotle and their teaching philosophy at the Lyceum in Athens, uses different appellations and calls the Lyceum the house of education, "Dar al-Ta'leem".[17] For instance, fourteenth-century historian and geographer Abulfeda (d. 1331) in his well-known book *Taqwim al-Buldan* refers to Athens as the city of Greek philosophers that is to say the "Dar al-Hikma" of the Greeks.[18]

Obviously, tenth-century authors and those in the following periods, other than al-Nadim, were using the generic name of Bayt al-Hikma, which was previously coined for the libraries of Abbasid Caliphs, for pre-Islamic royal libraries. Its synonym *Dar al-Hikma*, connoting a wider place or meaning a seat of wisdom, was used for Athens, which they considered an important seat of philosophy and the sciences of the ancients.

In an attempt to further elaborate on the history of coinage of the appellation the House of Wisdom, it is rather a rewarding exercise to compare two texts related to the same book written at different times. This comparison provides an important clue to the emergence and development of the appellation of Bayt al-Hikma as an Arabic terminology for the royal library. Ibn al-Muqa'fa (d. around 756), the famous author and translator, who came from Persian descent and pioneer of Arabic literary prose, translated the famous collection of tables from Indian roots known as *Kalila and Dimna* from Pahlavi into Arabic.[19] In this book, there is an autobiographical introduction written by Buzoe for the translation of the book from Sanskrit to Pahlavi. Buzoe was a physician who was sent to India by the Sassanian King Khusrav Anusharwan (r. 531–579) in search of this famous book. Ibn al-Muqa'fa translated the voyage and adventures of Buzoe in India, which included references to the library of the Indian king. Here, Ibn al-Muqa'fa refers to the royal libraries as "*khaza'in*" which is the plural of "*khizana*".[20]

The second text is an introduction of extraneous origin and ascribed to a certain Bahnud Ibn Sahwan, also known as Ali Ibn al-Shah al-Farisi, where he gives an account of the history of the book in India. French orientalist De Sacy (d. 1838) published this introduction together with the text of al-Muqa'fa. However, this introduction is not found in the oldest four manuscripts of the Arabic text; most probably it was added later. The date this introduction was written is not yet established but it is clear that it was written long after Ibn al-Muqa'fa's time and was included in some later manuscripts. Here, the short form of khizana/khazan'in was not used in referring to the library of the Indian kings, as was the case in the early authentic text, which Ibn al-Muqa'fa translated from Pahlavi.[21]

Instead, the appellations *Khazain al-Hikma* and *Bayt al-Hikma* are used here.[22] We may conclude that during the time the second introduction was written, the terms "Bayt al-Hikma" and "Khazinat al-Hikma" were already developed as compound names for the royal library. They were used after the death of Ibn al-Muqa'fa in the middle of the second century AH/eighth century CE. They were used frequently in this context when the introduction attributed to Ali b. al-Shah al-Farisi was written.

As an antithesis to Youssef Eche's Greek allusion, Dimitri Gutas in his study on *Greek Thought and Arabic Culture* assumes that "in the first place, Bayt al-Hikma as a term is the translation of the Sassanian designation of a library".[23] This assumption is advanced in a context where he tries to relate this institution to what he considers as the attempts of the Iranian bureaucrats of the early Abbasid epoch to restore the Sassanid administrative and bureaucratic setup and recover the Sassanid imperial ideology. The discussion of this assumption falls outside the scope of this study; however, what should be emphasized in this context is that, while Gutas negates the affiliation of Bayt al-Hikma with Greek legacy, he tries to establish its relation to a pre-Islamic Persian past. As implied evidence for such an assumption, he quotes a sentence mentioned in a book on poetic proverbs entitled *Kitab al-Amthal al-Sadira 'an Buyut al-shi'r* written by Hamza al-Isfahani (d. after 360/970).[24] The manuscript of this book consists of an introduction, two divisions, the first divisions consist of seven *bab*s and these comprise 60 *fasl*s while the second division is composed of seven topics (fen). al-Isfahani elaborates on the Arabic poetic proverbs and states that in this context the Arabs have preceded other nations to which he makes short references. In his reference to Greeks, he says that their liking for poetry was less than that of the Arabs and Persians and refers to the Greek scholars' poetic quotations in their writings. He mentions Aristotle who liked poetry and quoted Homer. He also refers to Plato who did not like poetry and considered that poets and painters were deceived by their ears and eyes respectfully. Al-Isfahani had a collection of 4700 Arabic distiches and hemistiches that became proverbs among the ancients Arabs and approximately 400 proverbs were translated from Persian to Arabic. In mentioning poems in pre-Islamic Iran, he says the books that contained Persian lore, war reports and various pieces of information about famous lovers that were originally composed in prose, were recast in poetry for the [Sassanid] Kings. In this context, al-Isfahani continues to say that these poems were written in books that were to be "kept forever in the repositories (khaza'in), which were houses of wisdom" (tudawwan fi butun al-kutub wa tukhallad fi al-khaza'in allatî kanat buyut al-hikma). Al-Isfahani concludes by saying, "With the decline of their state, most of these books were lost; however more than ten thousand folios of writings and poems in Persian were left behind".[25]

Gutas drew his above-mentioned assumption that Bayt al-Hikma as a term is the translation of Sasanian designation for a library and he notes, not from the unpublished manuscript of al-Isfahani's book but rather from "the summary information given by Gregor Schoeler".[26] It is obvious that al-Isfahani, while calling the Persian royal libraries "houses of wisdom", does not explicitly or implicitly refer to its Persian name or to the appellation Bayt al-Hikma as its Arabic translation. He was simply using the established name for a royal library in his time (tenth century).

Meanwhile, Ibn Hamza al-Isfahani, in his published book on the "History of Kings and Prophets", provides clear evidence about the interchangeable use of the term "Khizana" for the court library of al-Ma'mun. In the first chapter of his book, he refers to eight books on the history of Persian kings that he consulted and mentioned a certain book, which he says was copied from al-Ma'mun's library; "Khizanat al-Ma'mun".[27] It is clear that he calls this library after the death of its founder in the same manner al-Nadim does by saying Khizanat al-Ma'mun.

Our research could not locate any specific Pahlavi term that denotes the name for a royal library. Meanwhile, on the authority of scholars of Middle Iranian language such a term does not exist in surviving Pahlavi texts.[28] However, in support of his above-mentioned assumption in a later published article on the subject, D. Gutas and Kevin Van Bladel mention that the expression of Bayt al-Hikma (as well as the alternate expression, Khizanat al-Hikma) apparently is the Arabic translation of a middle Persian term *ganj* for "libraries of Sasanian kings". This assumption is based on a study of M. Shaki namely *the Denkard Account from the sixth century of History of the Zoroastrian Scriptures*, dated from middle of the sixth century.[29]

On his elaboration on the word *ganj* mentioned in this text from the sixth century, and its different readings, Shaki provides a

What Was the Abbasid Caliph's Library Called? 45

detailed discussion which does not reflect any similarity between the Arabic term of House of Wisdom and the Pahlavi term *ganj*. He clearly says

> ... These considerations apart, we do not know of any "satrapal" [the governors of the provinces of ancient Median and Achaemenid Empire] treasury or archives which, none the less, were rendered "royal" by the scholars who have accepted this reading. The oldest reference to such a state or royal archives is made by the Bible ... They preserved the Avesta and Zand which were both written in gold on cow hides in the Royal Treasury. Bôxtagân states that he deposited his ayâdgâr in the *ganj ı sahigan*, which shows that this Royal (Palace) Treasury was also used as archives.[30]

D. Gutas in his book *Greek Thought and Arabic Culture*, quotes this text of Denkard's book and endorses the explanations of Royal Treasury.[31]

It is obvious from this sixth-century Pahlavi text that the word *ganj* is used to denote the place where books or other archival material would be kept under the Sasanian rulers. However, this has nothing to do with the compound name of the Abbasid House of Wisdom. It is clear that *ganj* is equivalent to the Arabic Khizane, and at the same time the Greek thêkê, as both denote the place or the case where books are kept. Meanwhile, it is satisfactory to note that *ganj* in the new Iranian language means store, hoard, store house ... etc.,[32] one of the clear indications of the fact that the compound name in Arabic Bayt al-Hikma for the royal libraries was established and used in new Persian. A quotation from the eleventh century by the Persian poet Nasir Khusraw (d. after 1070) lamented "the old good days in Balkh" and says, "it was the House of Wisdom (Khane-e Hikmet) alas it turned to ruins".[33] This quotation clearly shows that the Arabic term was either used originally or as translated into Persian equivalent, "khane-e hikmet".

Al-Nadim, our main source on the Abbasid Bayt al-Hikma and scholarly activities related to pre-Islamic sciences, does not use this term for the libraries of ancient Persians. He quoted the famous astronomer and astrologer, Abu Ma'shar Ibn Muhammed Ibn 'Umar al-Balkhi (Albo Masar) (d. 886)[34] from his book on the variations of astronomical tables, on the eagerness of the Persian kings to collect and preserve books, but al-Nadim does not use any specific appellation for these libraries.[35] Al-Nadim, also quotes the words of Abu

Sahl [al-Fadl] Ibn Nawbakht (d. 815) on Dahhak Ibn Qay, one of the legendary rulers of Persia who was overthrown by Faridun;

> He [al-Dahhak] built a city in al-Sawad ... He gathered into it the science of the scholars and built there twelve palaces, according to the number of the signs of the zodiac, calling them by the names [of these signs]. He stored the scholars' books in them and caused the scholars themselves to live in them.[36]

It is well known that both sources of al-Nadim were close associates of the Abbasid court and surely, they knew well what the House of Wisdom was. Abu Sahl, the famous physician and astronomer, was at the court of Harun al-Rashid and Abu Ma'shar was considered one of the most learned scholars of his time on the history of pre-Islamic Persia and had a strong sense of the intellectual primacy of Iran among the nations of Eurasian continent. He was also the munajjim (astronomer-astrologer) of al-Muwaffaq (r. 875–91), brother of the Caliph al-Mu'tamid (870–892).

It is clear from the above quotation and similar examples that this term was not used specifically for Iranian libraries that could have easily competed with the Abbasid Bayt al-Hikma as far as their volume and collections are considered.

It is quite interesting that al-Nadim, who does not use the appellation House of Wisdom for ancient Persian Royal libraries while providing information about alchemists and the art of alchemy in ancient Egypt, uses the appellation Bayt al-Hikma in a different context. In the tenth and at the end of the last chapter of his *al-Fihrist*, it is stated:

> there were authors and learned men in this field among the people of Egypt where there was the beginning of talk about the Art and from which place, they derived it. The [well] known Barabi[37] which were the houses of wisdom and Mariyāh were in the land of Egypt.[38]

Meanwhile, it seems that as an expression denoting the royal libraries, the appellation Bayt al-Hikma was not universally endorsed by Arab authors of the period. For example, Ibn Juljul (944–994), the Andalusian contemporary of al-Nadim, in giving information about Abbasid physicians and philosophers in his biographical book, does not use this term but settles for "Khazain al-Kutup" for the libraries.[39] In the thirteenth century, al-Qıftî uses the term khizane/

khaza'in more frequently for the royal libraries, even for the great Alexandria library.[40] It is also noticeable that as time passed, its usage diminished and its Fatimid equivalent "Dar al-Hikma" came into use, as can be seen in the above example of al-Maqrizi in the fourteenth century.

From all the above examples and related discussions, it may be deduced that the term Bayt al-Hikma was not transferred from Greek and Persian but came out as a specific term for the royal library when it became larger, and when its contents were dominated by Hikma/Wisdom books. Contrary to the assumption of Eche, it did not appear in the Muawiya period and then disappear,[41] nor was it the Arabic translation of the name given to old Sassanid royal libraries as argued by D. Gutas. As we understand, the compound name Bayt al-Hikma was not an extant, generic name, but it was composed in the Abbasid period and used to identify the collections in the great library joined to the palace during the periods of Harun al-Rashid and al-Ma'mun. Here an extensive collection of books related to pre-Islamic sciences and their catalogues were kept in a large area consisting of more than one room where scholarly activities related to these sciences could have been conducted. The plausible influence of Sassanid court libraries on their Abbasid counterparts cannot be disclaimed offhand; however, it may be explained within the wider context of the Persian influence on the Abbasid institutions. We believe the primary sources at hand do not lend themselves to any assumption to determine this influence. However, we are now better informed about Sassanid royal libraries as will be seen in Part VI.

Notes

1 Sa'id al-Andalusi, *Science in the Medieval World, "Book of Categories on Nations"*, trans. and edited by Semaan I. Salem and Alok Kumar, Austin, University of Texas Press, 1991, p. 43.
2 Katip Çelebi, *Kashf al-Zunun*, edited by E. Ihsanoglu, B.A. Marouf, Al-Furqan Edition, London, 2021, Vol. 3, pp. 412–415.
3 Al-Mas'udi, *The Meadows of Gold*, trans. and edited by Paul Lunde and Caroline Stone, London, Kegan Paul, 1989, p. 388.
4 AN I, p. 373.
5 AN I, p. 25.
6 AN I, p. 374.
7 AN II, pp. 142, 215.
8 AN I, p. 374.
9 AN I, p. 177.
10 AN I, pp. 25, 326, 374; AN II, pp. 142, 215, 326, 466.
11 AN I, pp. 24, 234, 373; AN II, p. 235.

12 AN I, pp. 13, 14, 44.
13 Y. Eche, pp. 44–48
14 Hunain Ibn Ishaq, Adab al-Falasife (Sentences des Philosophers), Abbreviation par Mohamed Bin Ali Bin Ibrahim, Edition Critique, note et Introduction par Abdurrahman Badawi, publication de l'Institue de Manuscript Arabes, Kuwait, 1985, p. 49.
15 Ibn Hawqal, Suret al-Ard (The face of the Earth), Leiden, 1938, 2nd Edition, Vol. I, s. 202.
16 E.W. Lane, Vol. I, p. 931.
17 AN II, pp. 157, 158, 172.
18 İsmail bin Ali b. Mahmud b. Muhammed bin Umar b. Shahinshah bin Ayyub, Abulfeda, Géographie D'aboulféda, Kitab Taqwim al-Buldun, M. Reinaud and M. Le bon Mac Guckin de Slane (eds.), Paris, L'imprimerie Royale, 1840, pp. 210, 216.
19 Here De Sacy's edition of Kalila and Dimna will be used as it has the two introductions; however, it is not the best edition and is based on an inferior manuscript. Silvestre De Sacy, Calila et Dimna ou Fables De Bidpai, Paris, De L'imprimerie Royale, 1816.
20 De Sacy, pp. 33, 34.
21 On the introduction of Ali bin al-Shah al-Farisi; see De Sacy, p. 15 f.n. 1; Theodor Nöldeke, Die Erzahlun von Mausekönig und seinen Ministern, Göttingen, Dieterich'sche Verlags-Buchhandlung, 1879, pp. 6, 7; A.F.L. Beeston, "The 'Ali Ibn Shah' Preface to Kalilah wa Dimnah", Oriens Journal, Vol. VII, 1954, p. 81; Carl Brockelmann, "Kalīla wa Dimna", EI², IV, 1978, pp. 503–506.
22 De Sacy, pp. 25–31.
23 D. Gutas, pp. 54, 55.
24 Ibid.
25 Hamza Al-Isfahani, Kitab al-Amthal al-Sadira 'an Buyut al-shi'r, Berlin manuscript, or. quart. n. 1215, ff.1a-6b.
26 Gutas, p. 55, fn. 45; Gregor Schoeler, Arabische Handschriften, Tell II, Stutgart F. Steiner, 1990, p. 308.
27 The Arabic text of al-Isfahani's book was first published with the Latin translation made by J.M.E. Gottwaldt (ed.) Hamzae Ispahanensis, Kitab Tarikh Siniy Muluk al-Ard wa al-Anbiya, Annalium, Libri X, Lipsiae, 1848, pp. 8, 9. For al-Isfahani, see Rosenfeld-Ihsanoglu, No. 196.
28 Personal communication with the Prof. Touraj Danyaee from California State University, Fullerton, 2003.
29 Kevin Bladel, "Bayt al-Hikma", Encyclopedia of Islam, Third Edition, Leiden, Brill, 2009, s. 133–137.
30 Mansour Shaki, "The Denkard Account of History of the Zoroastrrian Scriptures", Archiv Orientalni, Praha, Vol. 49, 1981, pp. 114–125.
31 D. Gutas, p. 36.
32 F. Steingass, Persian – English Dictionary, 6th Edition, Routledge, s. 1098.
33 Mahdi Muhakqiq, "Risalet Hunayn Ibn Ishaq", in (the Book of collection of Papers delivered on the 1200th Anniversary of the Foundation of Bayt al-Hikma) Bayt al-Hikma al-Abbasi: A'rakat al-Madi ve Ru'yat al-Hadır, Baghdad, Bayt al-Hikma Institution Publishing, Vol. 2, 2001, p. 176.
34 Rosenfeld-Ihsanoglu, No. 88.
35 AN II, pp. 135–137; B. Dodge, pp. 576–678.

36 AN II, pp. 131–135; B. Dodge, p. 573.
37 Barabi plural Barba in Arabic, meaning old temples and monuments, see Gaston Wiet, "Barbā", in *Encyclopedia of Islam*, Second Edition, Leiden, Brill, 2012.
38 AN II, p. 466; Dodge, p. 868, in the Arabic text of al-Nadim, her refers to the Egyptian Barabi as Buyut al-Hikma (houses of Wisdom); however, Dodge translate the term as the houses of learning.
39 Ibn Juljul, p. 61.
40 al-Qıfti, Leipzig, p. 355.
41 Y. Eche, p. 17.

Part VI Was the House of Science an Arena for Debates?

Another issue related to the function of the House of Wisdom is its depiction as a place of meetings and arena of debates among scholars. Primary sources and modern studies have no historiographical problem with al-Ma'mun's support of the theology of the Mu'tazila creed on the createdness of the Qur'an. It is also established that he enjoyed debates on this subject and many others, thanks to his keen interest in other scholarly issues. However, it looks like the essential problem here is to attribute all these activities to the House of Wisdom. A clear example of this is the way Y. Eche extrapolated the meaning of certain accounts. For instance, he interprets the statement of Ibn Taghribirdi (d. 1470) that al-Ma'mun "brought closer to him the theologians" to "al-Ma'mun installed them in the House of Wisdom" and to claim that a number of them dwelled in the House of Wisdom.[1] According to Eche, it was not only the theologians who were given accommodation there but there were also astrologers and other scholars.

It is clear from Sa'id al-Andalusi's book that among al-Ma'mun's diversified interest in intellectual matters and his keen patronage for scholars that "he provided a special audience for the scientists, listened to what they had to say, enjoyed their discussions [and debates] and showered them with favour".[2] There are several accounts supporting Sa'id al-Andalusi's statement. But these accounts obviously do not say that these discussions took place at the House of Wisdom but in his *Majlis* (the lounge where guests were received, can sit and converse) at his palace. Ibn Taghribirdi, the famous Mamluk era historian, narrates that "in 209/824 al-Ma'mun brought closer the theologians (ehl al-kelam) and ordered them to debate in his presence" then he mentions the names of some scholars who were supporters of the createdness of the Qur'an including above-mentioned al-Marisi.[3]

The first scholar to advance the claim that these debates took place at the House of Wisdom was Y. Eche.[4] He, with some prudence, tells

Was the House of Science an Arena for Debates? 51

the story of a long debate between Abd al-Aziz al-Kinani (d. 240/854), a staunch opponent to the createdness of Qur'an and Bishr al-Marisi (d. 218/833) the vocal supporter and advocate of this cause. This debate according to Y. Eche's interpretation took place at the House of Wisdom in the presence of Caliph al-Ma'mun as Eche quotes at length from a book attributed to al-Kinani, the *Kitab al-Hayda*, a hitherto unpublished manuscript.[5] In novelistic style, the book presents a detailed and colorful account on the voyage of al-Kinani from Mecca to Baghdad and his search for Bishr al-Marisi to challenge him and invite him for debate. Al-Kinani narrates that after arriving to Baghdad, he made a public statement against the claim of the createdness of the Qur'an after a Friday prayer in the congressional mosque. He was interrogated by al-Ma'mun's people, and the caliph agreed to hold a debate between him and al-Marisi. Eche tells us, while referring to the Damascus manuscript of the book, that scholars from different disciplines and diverse opinions came together in the House of Wisdom where al-Ma'mun was following the debate behind a curtain. Here we find a discrepancy between what Eche quotes based on the Zahiriye manuscript and the edited text of al-Hayda book based on four manuscripts including the Zahirriyye one.[6] Eche says that al-Ma'mun held weekly *Majlis* on Fridays in the House of Wisdom. However, the published text clearly says that there were two debates, the first was held on Monday but not specifically in the House of Wisdom but in the hall of the Palace of the Caliph (Dar Amir al-Mu'minin) and the second was on a Friday again not in the House of Wisdom, as will be explained below.

Al-Kinani describes his attendance of the first debate on a Monday and tells us that he was taken to the Palace of al-Ma'mun accompanied by officials taking charge of him. Then he describes going through corridors from one to another. Later they arrived at the courtyard which was crowded by people and arms. When he reached the door of the hall (iwan) and the curtain was removed, he started to hear the caliph's voice saying "let him come closer ... let him come closer". Then al-Ma'mun ordered the debate to commence between him and Bishr al-Marisi where al-Ma'mun personally participated in the discussions. The opponents of al-Kinani provoked the caliph to have a second debate claiming that Kinani leaked the details of the debate to the public and put the caliph in an unfavorable situation. So, the narrative of al-Hayda book's goes; opponents brought their concerns to al-Ma'mun in his Majlis where he would meet the scholars of jurisprudence, Arabic literature, and philosophical theology (ahl al-Nazar wa al-Kalam) in the House of Wisdom on Fridays.[7]

According to al-Kinani, they managed to convince the caliph to have a second debate saying that he has written a book on the subject. So, the caliph summoned him to the palace. At this point al-Kinani says that in the Palace, in a place "other than the House of Wisdom", the second debate took place.[8]

It is very obvious that the two debates did not take place in the House of Wisdom. The first was at a hall (Iwan), where the caliph used to have his regular Majlis and the second was at a place identified as "other than the House of Wisdom". The debates between al-Kinani and al-Marisi are reported in many sources; however, they do not identify the place where the debates were conducted, whether they were at the House of Wisdom or not was not confirmed.

An important clue in al-Kinani's account that the first draft of his book was a summary of the first debate occupies ten pages.[9] It seems that the extant, long text was expounded by his supporters and followers later on and this might have raised the doubts of outstanding scholars such as al-Zehebi (d. 1274), al-Subki (d. 1327), and others with regard to the authenticity of the book.[10] This is why indirect, roundabout references to the House of Wisdom in the text could be added later and not by the author in its first draft. Hence this sole indirect reference to the House of Wisdom should be treated carefully. One can conclude from this that the debates related to the createdness of Qur'an, did in fact take place in the presence and the participation of al-Mamun but this was not in the library called House of Wisdom, but in different parts of the Palace.

Our purpose here is not to discuss the substance of the above-mentioned debate about the createdness of the Qur'an or related philosophical and religious implications but rather about the relevance of this narrative to the functions of the House of Wisdom and to clarify if the House of Wisdom was a place where scholars engaged in debates in the presence of caliph or not. The bone of contention for us here is not the hair-splitting philosophical and religious discussions but rather to establish that the House of Wisdom was not, as has been claimed, a conference hall for such gatherings of scholars and to indicate that such activities would be in the caliph's palace as it was the custom in his (*Majlis*).

The second claim related to the House of Wisdom as a place of meeting of scholars was made by Balty-Gueston.[11] She quotes Hunayn Ibn Ishaq and interprets his very explicit statement on Greek philosophers erroneously. Hunayn Ibn Ishaq, who wrote the oldest surviving Arabic text comprising maxims and aphorisms of Greek philosophers, makes no mention whatsoever in this text to the Abbasid House of Wisdom. The available text is an abridgment made by a certain Mohamed Ibn Ali bin Ali bin Ibrahim bin Ahmed bin Mohamed al-Ansari, who is not a well-known author.[12] This text is a book on Greek philosophers and philosophy. Besides maxims and aphorisms, it contains detailed accounts on the meetings of philosophers during Greek festivities. Hunayn gives explanations under the title of "the meetings of philosophers in the Houses of Wisdom in the festivities and their discussions about wisdom". Hunayn, in his introductory remarks to this chapter, clearly qualifies the festivities as the Greek festivities. In these accounts he mentions different groups of philosophers, ranging from 4 to 13, held meetings to discuss issues related to philosophy and the legacy of the founders of wisdom. Hunayn in his seven accounts of these meetings clearly says that one of them was held in the House of Wisdom. As for the other meetings he mentions that one of them was in the marble temple, *Haykel al-Rukham*[13] then he names places like the house of gold, *Bayt al-Zahab*,[14] or the vault of the Kings *Sirdab al-Muluk*[15] or the house of golden images *Bayt al-Suwar al-Mudhahhabe*.[16] In one of these accounts he mentions that four philosophers; a Greek, an Indian, a Byzantine, and Persian met in the Majlis of King Luqianus where they had to answer the King's question about what is eloquence.[17] Hunayn in another context refers to a legend that the King built a House of Wisdom for his son and asked Aristotle, who was a young orphan then, to be in the service of his son who would be educated by Plato.[18] It is obvious that Hunayn does not refer to the Abbasid House of Wisdom at any rate. His book is mainly on the Greek context with the exception of the meeting held in the presence of the King Luqianus which possibly did not take place in Hellenic times but the late Hellenistic era and his reference to a meeting in the presence of Sasanian King Anusharwan/Khosrow I. Abd al-Rahman Badawi, in his introduction to Hunayn's book, reflects on the origin of this book and he favors German orientalists' opinions that it was compiled from Greek-Byzantine sources. In our opinion this explains the reference to Anusharwan, besides other issues mentioned in the introduction.

In his reference to the House of Wisdom, Hunayn certainly refers to an institution where philosophers would meet either to teach philosophy or to have discussions or a kind of library where books of wisdom/philosophy would be available.

Since the Greek texts that Hunayn compiled his book from are not known to us, it is difficult to find out what was the Greek equivalent of the Arabic Bayt al-Hikma/House of Wisdom. What is clear for us here is that Hunayn was using the compound name of House of

Wisdom which was known to him, meaning that it was a place where philosophy was taught or discussed.

Balty-Gueston in her article on the House of Wisdom refers to Hunayn's book and its chapter on "the meeting of philosophers in the Houses of Wisdom in the festivities and their discussions about wisdom". Despite the explicit Greek context, she erroneously considers Hunayn's reference to Bayt al-Hikma as relating to the Abbasid institution. She concludes, referring to the discussions in Baghdad without any reasoning, saying "this function emerges closely under the reign of al-Ma'mun and it seems at this moment that Bayt al-Hikma played a role in discussions prior to the diffusion of Mu'tazilaism".[19]

To conclude on these issues, we can state that the public debates like the one that took place between al-Kinani and al-Marisi – if it is really happened – were conducted in the palace wherever the caliph would convene his *Majlis*, consequently the House of Wisdom was not an arena of debates. Nevertheless, it was a place where the Mu'tazila scholars would meet and consult philosophy books and may have had circles of discussions among themselves.

Another claim about the House of Wisdom being a center of Shu'ubizm (Shu'ubiyya), a movement within the early Muslim society which denied any privileged position of the Arabs. This movement which started asking for equality among all Muslims, later developed as a claim of non-Arab supremacy.[20]

Eche, making a reference to Sahl bin Harun the director of the House of Wisdom and other senior associates of the House of Wisdom including Allan Ibn Hassan al-Warraq who was also known as Allan al-Shu'ubi, being all from Persian origin and newly convert to the Islam and known to be proponents of Shu'ubizm. He concludes saying "are these not suggestive facts which leads us to believe the Bayt al-Hikma could have been a Shu'ubiya center?"[21]

Fortunately, this claim did not find too much support and was not carried on in secondary literature.[22]

Notes

1 Y. Eche, pp. 53, 54.
2 Sa'id al-Andalusi, p. 44.
3 Ibn Tahgribirdi, *al-Nujum al-zahira fi muluk Misr wa-l-Qahira*, Vol. 2, Cairo, Dar al-Kulub al-Mısırriyye, 1950, p. 187.
4 Y. Eche, pp. 50, 51; for far fetching exaggerations on this aspect see for instance, Attallah's book, pp. 182–185.
5 Kitab al-Hayda, Zahiriyye Manuscript Collection, Damascus, Tassawuf No. 129, f.67-b (quoted by Y. Eche, p. 48).

Was the House of Science an Arena for Debates? 55

6 Abd al-Aziz al-Kinani, *Kitab Al-Hayda*, edited by Jamil Saliba, Damascus, Arab Academy, 1964.
7 Al-Hayda, part one and part two, J. Saliba's edition.
8 Ibid., 3rd Part, 146–226.
9 Ibid., 146–226.
10 Ibid., the Editor's introduction, pp. 17–23; Ibn al-Subki, *Tabaqat al-Shefiyye*, Cairo, 1323, Vol. I, pp. 265, 266.
11 Marie Genevieve Balty-Gueston, "Le Bayt al-Hikm de Baghdad", *Arabica Journal*, Vol. 39, 1992, pp. 138, 139.
12 Hunain Ibn Ishaq, Adab al-Falasife, pp. 15–19. The published text is a careful critical edition out of four manuscripts including a detailed introduction by the editor Abd al-Rahman Badawi published in 1985.
13 Ibid., p. 57.
14 Ibid., p. 56.
15 Ibid., p. 58.
16 Ibid., p. 48.
17 Ibid., p. 56.
18 Ibid., pp. 51, 52.
19 Balty Gueston, pp. 138, 139.
20 S. Enderwitz, "Shu'ubiyya", *Encyclopedia of Islam*, Vol. 9, Leiden, Brill, 1997, pp. 513, 514.
21 Y. Eche, p. 59.
22 Balty-Gueston, does not favor this claim, 1994, p. 283.

Part VII What Was the Reality?

The myth of the House of Wisdom as previously explained was the outcome of a wild exaggeration and maximalist approach. Meanwhile, the unavailability of detailed historical accounts and the scanty information at hand do not make it an easy task to draw an accurate picture of this ninth-century palace library.

The actual picture that emerges from careful examination of the available short references clearly tells us about the existence of an organized palace library during the reign of both Abbasid Caliphs Harun al-Rashid and his son al-Ma'mun. Two important surviving historical accounts related to them include many clues that assert certain aspects of the existence, function, and working manners of this library as well as shed light on how the two caliphs made use of their library. Here below is the full English translation of these accounts for the benefit of wider readership.

The first account relates to the prominent Arab philologist al-Asma'i (d. 828) who narrated:

> It was the habit of the Imam Caliph Haroun al-Rashid, when he feels spirited and lively to call me to narrate to him the chronicles of past nations and bygone centuries. It happened that as I was narrating to him one night, he asked me "al-Asma'i, where are the former Kings and their sons?" I answered him by saying "Prince of the Faithful, they have gone to their destiny". At this point the Caliph raised his hands towards the sky and said "O, Annihilator of Kings, have mercy on me when you join me to them". Then he called Saleh the keeper of his prayer hall and told him "go to the director of the 'House of Wisdom" and ask him to fetch the [book] *"Siyar al-Muluk"* [Biographies of Kings] and bring it to me.

What Was the Reality? 57

The director brought the book. The caliph asked al-Asma'i to read from it, so he read to him six chapters from the book that night. At this point, the caliph told him to go to al-Buhturi (the Jurist Judge) to help him in writing the events of the epoch between Adam and Sam, the son of Noah".[1]

The second account that deserves attention is what al-Qayrawani (d. 1060) reports from the celebrated Arab prose writer al-Jahiz (d. 869) who quotes al-Hasan Ibn Sahl Ibn Nawbakht, by saying

> al-Hasan ibn Sahl related to me that Caliph al-Ma'mun once asked: "Which of the books by Arabs is the noblest?" I said "al-Mubt'da' [The Commencement]". He said "No", I said "Then, it's the book of History". He again said "No". Then he paused and said that it is the book of the interpretation of the Qur'an, because the Qur'an is immaculate, and its interpretation is immaculate too. Then he asked "Which of the books by non-Arabs [al-'Ajam] is the noblest among them?" I cited many names [of books], but he said "the book of *Jawadan Khired [Mortal Wisdom]* is the noblest among them." At this point he asked me for the catalogue of non-Arab books, but he did not find any mentions of that book in the catalogue. Then he said, "How come that the name of that book does not figure in the catalogue?" I said, "This is the book of Dhouban and I wrote part of it". He said "Bring it to me quickly!" I asked a messenger to bring it and when the messenger returned, the Caliph was up for prayer. Seeing me coming back carrying the book, the Caliph stopped the prayer, took the book and started to read from it. Whenever he finishes reading a Chapter, he says "There is no God but God".
>
> Getting tired, he sat down and continued to read. I told him the prayer has a fixed time that elapses while reading has no fixed time. He answered me "you are right but I was afraid to be distracted from focusing on my prayers thinking in my heart about the delights of the content of this book. I find no remedy to distraction except by mentioning death". Then he started to recite from the Koran "Verily, you are bound to die, and they are bound to die too" (Surat Az-Zumar No: 39 [The Throngs] Verse 30]. Then he put down the book, stood up and started to pray. Upon completing his prayer, he again took the book and resumed reading until he read it all. Then he asked me "Where is the rest of the book?", I answered "It remained with Dhouban, who did not give it to me.". At this point he told me "Covenant is a rope, one of its

two ends is in the hand of God and the second end is in our hands; otherwise, I would have taken that book. This, by God, is the talk that counts, and not what we are uttering by our tongues in the apertures of our mouth".[2]

These two accounts substantiate the existence of the library close to the dwellings of the caliph and show as well that its director was on duty in the time his services were needed even in late times of the day. Then they show that Harun al-Rashid and al-Ma'mun had their habits of reading, listening, and discussing books with their companions. The second report of al-Jahiz tells us for the first time that there were catalogues of the library collection. They were known to al-Ma'mun and he asked for one of them that was the catalogue of non-Arab (Ajam) books. This implies that there was another catalogue of Arab books, and perhaps of Greek books and probably other catalogues.

There are two surviving accounts from the tenth century that show how large libraries and collections were organized. These accounts support our opinion on the content of the Abbasid palace library. The first account belongs to the Buyid ruler of Fars, 'Adud al-Dawla (d. 977) who set up a splendid library in his palace in Shiraz described by al-Muqaddisi (d. 991):

> There is a manager, a librarian and a supervisor from among the people of good repute in the town and there was not a book written up to that time, of all the various sciences, but happened to be there. It consists of a long oblong gallery in a large hall with rooms on every side. He attached to all the walls of the gallery and rooms bookcases six feet in height and three cubits long, made of wood and decorated ... For every subject there are bookcases and catalogues in which are the names of the book.[3]

The second account related to the prominent philosopher, physician, and polymath scholar Avicenna (980–1037) who describes the library established by the Samanids in Bukhara which he used intensely:

> a building with many rooms in each of which were chests of books opposite each other. In one room, there were books on Arabic language and poetry, in another jurisprudence and each room was similarly [dedicated] to a single science.[4]

As clearly described the big libraries had their collection of books well arranged and organized according to their subject and had catalogues to help their readers.

A The Origin of Book Collections

What Was the Reality? 59

Acquiring books in the early Abbasid era should have been a demanding task for any librarian particularly before the advent of paper to the capital Baghdad. Nevertheless, acquiring books for the caliphal library would be more challenging where they were expected to collect these books from different sources all over. Besides the primary interests of the caliphs and scholars under their patronage, there were, for a decade after the founding of Baghdad as the new Abbasid capital, some members of their entourage who were undoubtedly behind the growing of this collection. In addition to the diversified sources mentioned above we should underline the introduction of paper manufacturing and using paper as a material for the production of books. The widespread adoption of paper manufacturing boosted the easy and cheap production of books.

The Ottoman bibliographer and polymath Katip Çelebi (d. 1657), in his universal bibliography *Kashf al-Zunun* and in reference to his predecessors, narrates that it was al-Mansur the second Abbasid Caliph who asked the Byzantine emperor to send him books and that the emperor sent him Euclid's book and other books on mathematics.[5]

Primary sources at hand are explicit about the interest of both caliphs, Harun al-Rashid and his son al-Ma'mun, in locating Greek books inside their empire's vast land or neighboring Byzantian Empire. Ibn Juljul and many others who followed him like Ibn al-Qifti and Ibn Abi Useybia narrated that Harun al-Rashid ordered Yuhanna Ibn Masawayh to translate the ancient medical books that were found in Ankara, Amuriye [Amorium], and Byzantine lands that became part of the Abbasid Empire.[6]

Notwithstanding the debate on the authenticity of this narrative and whether or not Ibn Masawayh started his career as translator during Harun al-Rashid or al-Ma'mun reigns, the substance of this narrative is historically correct. It is clear that Harun al-Rashid was interested in collecting ancient books to be recovered from Greek legacy.[7]

Despite the fact that the above-mentioned primary sources did not mention where the books collected from Ankara, Amorium, or elsewhere were deposited, it would be historically correct to say that they were added to the collection of palace library.

Al-Nadim, in his account on al-Ma'mun's keen interest in collecting and translating books related to pre-Islamic sciences, narrates the following:

> Between al-Ma'mun and the Byzantine emperor there was correspondence, for al-Ma'mun had sought aid opposing him. He

wrote to the Byzantine emperor asking the permission to obtain a selection of old scientific (manuscripts) stored and treasured in the Byzantine country. After first refusing, he complied with this. Accordingly, al-Ma'mun sent forth a group of men among whom were al-Hajjaj, Ibn Matar, Ibn al-Batriq, Salm, *Sahib* (director) of Bayt al-Hikma and others besides them. He brought the books selected from what they had found. Upon bringing them to him, he ordered to translate, so they made the translation.[8]

In this paragraph, we can see a direct connection with the Bayt al-Hikma by mentioning the name of its director, Salm. Despite the fact that there is no explicit mention that the books were collected for the Bayt al-Hikma, it goes without saying that these books would have eventually been deposited there.

Ibn Nubata al-Masri (d. 1366) tells us that al-Ma'mun became aware of the existence of a library containing Greek philosophers' works kept in Cyprus and that it was closed and not accessible. Al-Ma'mun kept good relations with the ruler of Cyprus and asked him to send this library. The ruler of Cyprus summoned his advisors and asked their opinion, and with one exception they all were against accepting al-Ma'mun's request. The bishop who was in favor of sending these books was of the opinion that "these rational sciences, wherever they were introduced, they distempered and provoked disagreement among scholars", so the narrative goes on that the ruler of Cyprus accepted the caliph's request, and the books were sent.[9]

Ibn Nubata also narrates that al-Ma'mun put Sahl bin Harun in charge of the repository of wisdom (Khizanat al-hikma) where books of philosophers transferred from Cyprus were kept.

The rationale behind this story is kind of an antirational school of thinking, nonetheless it indicates that al-Ma'mun was after Greek books all over.

B Patronage Associated with the Library

One of the well-documented examples of al-Ma'mun's patronage for scholars is the story of famous Arab grammarian Ibn al-Farra (d. 207/822) and his book *al-Hudud*. The report handed down to us by al-Khatib al-Baghdadi (d. 1071) in his famed book on the history of Baghdad indicates that Ibn al-Farra, upon approaching al-Ma'mun, received instructions to write a book that would compile the principles of Arabic grammar. Al-Ma'mun also allocated a special place for him at the Domicile (al-dar) and delegated slave maids and servants

What Was the Reality? 61

to attend to all his needs so that he may not endure any yearnings or feelings of estrangement. There were people even to keep him informed of the prayer times, scribes to record what he dictated, and still others to meet his financials needs, until he finished compiling the book *al-Hudud* after two years, which al-Ma'mun ordered to be copied and kept in libraries (khaza'in), then he was allowed to mix with people.[10] This account is an example of the ideal and comprehensive patronage and care to which any scholars aspires so that he may dedicate himself to authorship.

The text of al-Khatib al-Baghdadi includes two terms that are worthy of a particular pause, namely "al-dar" (domicile) and the "khaza'in" (repositories). The word "al dar" with the definite article is bound to refer to a particular place.[11] It is an abbreviation of Dar al Khilafa (The caliph's residence of Dar al-Ma'mun). This would mean that al-Ma'mun had allocated a special place for Ibn al-Farra in his own palace or its annexes. There is ample indication in the text also that al-Ma'mun provided him with all that one may require to dedicate oneself to scholarly work, along with servants, scribes, and caretakers, all of which cannot be housed together in the palace library. Once he was through with the book's craft, the caliph made a point of having it reproduced in several copies to be kept in libraries. Despite this clear narrative, there is a tendency in contemporary writings to state that such scholarly activities were carried on within the House of Wisdom.[12] There are other examples in biographical sources that show the generous allocations made by the caliph to scholars covering their needs, providing them premises full of facilities and awarding them after completing their work. The nonexistent mention of the House of Wisdom in these accounts does not mean categorically the absence of an institutional involvement. Nevertheless, in order to confirm and to have a definite opinion on this subject and other activities related to the House of Wisdom, new sources should be explored. The unique example of the tutoring of the three brothers of Banu Musa in the House of Wisdom upon the instructions of al-Ma'mun (see Part III) stands as proof of a possibility of providing this source of education under the roof of the House of Wisdom.

C The Library and Greek Books

Dimitri Gutas in his aforementioned study touches upon this institution and its place in Abbasid cultural life; he rightly argues that due to limited historical information, it is wrong to envisage Bayt al-Hikma as "something grandiose or significant, hence a minimalist

62 What Was the Reality?

interpretation would fit the historical record better". Meanwhile, he maintains that it was certainly not a center for the translation of Greek works into Arabic and the Greco-Arabic translation movement was completely unrelated to its other activities. Gutas built this assumption on the basis that Bayt al-Hikma was a library and, as an institution, it was part of the Sassanid administrative and bureaucratic state apparatus that was adapted under the early Abbasids around the concept of the "recovery" of the Sassanid imperial ideology.[13]

It is also true that Sassanid Persian customs were followed in the Abbasid Court ceremonies and government administration since Arabic traditions could not provide any relevant models. However, the well-known facts about the Persianate character of the Abbasid bureaucracy and the administrators of Bayt al-Hikma, who were, as we are aware, mainly of Persian origin, does not preclude the diversification of its activities. Our main source on Bayt al-Hikma has some clear evidences to the contrary. In his account on Ptolemy's *Almagest*, al-Nadim provides us with an explicit example about the involvement of Bayt al-Hikma's director in translating Greek books that was initiated by the Iranian vizier Yahya bin Khalid al-Barmaki. He reports that:

> The first person to become interested in translating and issuing it (Ptolemy's *Almagest*) in Arabic was Yahyâ Ibn Khâlid Ibn Barmak. A group of people explained it for him but as they did not understand it perfectly, he was not satisfied with it; so he called upon Abu Hassan and Salm, the director of Bayt al-Hikma, for explanation. They made sure [of its meaning] and persevered in making it accurate, after having summoned the best translators, tested their translation, and making sure of its good literary style and accuracy.[14]

To stress Bayt al-Hikma's role on the subject of Greek books, it should be emphasized that Salm, in addition to his duties as the director, was a member of the delegation that was sent to Byzantium by al-Ma'mun to collect Greek books. His presence as a member of the delegation illustrates his personal as well as institutional engagement.

In the following paragraph, al-Nadim relates al-Ma'mun's interest in this subject by narrating the caliph's famous dream in which he saw Aristotle.

> Al-Ma'mun saw in a dream the likeness of a man white in color, with a ruddy complexion, broad forehead, joined eyebrows,

What Was the Reality? 63

bald head, bloodshot eyes and good qualities sitting on his bed. Al-Ma'mun related "It was as though I was in front of him, filled with fear of him. Then I said, who are you?" He replied, "I am Aristotle." Then I was delighted with him and said, "Oh sage, may I ask you a question?" He said, "Ask it." Then I asked, "What is good?" He replied, "What is good in the law" I said "Then what next?" He replied "mind." I said again "Then what is next?" He replied, "What is good with the What is good with the public." I said, "Then what more?" He answered "More? There is no more." According to another quotation: "I [al-Ma'mun] said "give me something more!" He [Aristotle] replied "Whosoever gives you advice about gold, let him be for you like gold; and for you is oneness [of Allah]."[15]

According to the al-Nadim,

> this dream was one of the most definite reasons for the output of books. Between al-Ma'mun and the Byzantine emperor, there was correspondence, for al-Ma'mun had sought aid opposing him (*perhaps literally it should be "had overpowered him"*). Then he wrote to the Byzantine emperor asking his permission to obtain a selection of old scientific [manuscripts], stored and treasured in the Byzantine country. After first refusing, the emperor complied with this request. Accordingly, al-Ma'mun sent forth a group of men, among whom were al-Hajjaj Ibn Matar, Ibn al-Batriq, Salm, the director of the Bayt al-Hikma, and others besides them. They brought the books selected from among what they had found. Upon bringing them to him [al-Ma'mun], he ordered them to translate [the manuscripts] so that they made the translation.[16]

These above-mentioned quotations that acknowledge the involvement of Bayt al-Hikma's directors both in collecting the books from Byzantium and Cyprus and being charged by their translation exemplifies the scope and diversity of their duties that also included dealing with different aspects of the Greek books. This in contrast to the comments made by D. Gutas that the library was not a place which stored, as part of its mission, Greek manuscripts.[17] Though there is no explicit information in the primary sources at hand showing a direct connection between the translation movement as a whole and the assumption that Bayt al-Hikma was also a "translation center", it may easily be said that Greek books were collected from various places under the personal attention and auspices of Abbasid Caliphs, specifically al-Mansur, Harun al-Rashid, and al-Ma'mun; they were copied, bound, and preserved at Bayt al-Hikma, while only part of them would have been translated there. As explained in detail in Part III, the translations made from different languages did not have to be in a specific place as it was the case with other compilations and writings, it could be anywhere that provided the facility for scholarly working.

The accounts mentioned above show that the director's supervision of the translation of Ptolemy's *Almagest* was made under the patronage of Khalid bin Yahya, the Persian vizier of Harun al-Rashid who came from the famous Barmakid family. It clearly displays the director's active participation in the delegation that went to Byzantium during al-Ma'mun's reign. It is also a well-established fact that Salm, the Director of Bayt al-Hikma, was personally involved in translating Persian books[18] and we also need to mention that Sahl bin Harun was of Persian origin.

Stating that Bayt al-Hikma was an institution where some of the translations and compilations from Persian and Greek sources were made is correct statement. However, apart from these examples, it is not possible to come across any strong evidence proving that all translated or written books, especially those mentioned by al-Nadim, were written or translated in the House of Wisdom during this period.[19] These baseless claims are put forward in some modern publications, examples of which were referred to in Part II. Though the majority of these books were translated or written under the auspices of and with the financial support of the caliphs and prominent statesmen and scholars, it may be surmised that authors or translators prepared them in their own working premises. It is possible that translation activities were carried out in an organized way and there are hints and references that suggest the possibility of their having a connection with Bayt al-Hikma. Al-Qifti in his biography of Hunayn Ibn Ishaq narrates that he sat down (qa'ada) among the translators to translate [Greek] books on wisdom to Syriac and Arabic.[20] The verb "qa'ada" in this context means that there was a place where these group of translators would sit and do translations. Undoubtedly, the House of Wisdom could be an appropriate place for such activities.

D Abbasid Caliphal Library and Persian Royal Libraries

For the moment we do not have enough information on the impact of the Persian royal library model and tradition in the early Abbasid era. However, we have an unequaled, detailed text on this subject that belongs to the twelfth century, surviving in a manuscript copied in 630/1232, that furnishes us with fascinating details.

Contrary to the very brief remarks and passing references in Hamza al-Isfahani's book *Kitab al-Amthal al-Sadira 'an Buyut al-shi'r* regarding the Persian royal libraries, a book of royal deportments attributed to Abu'l Hasan Ali bin Razin (c. twelfth century) devotes a whole chapter to the palace library and the functions of its librarian in the service of the king.[21] The author states that in preparing the book, he benefited from Buzurgmihr's and Muhammed bin al-Haris al-Tha'labi's (d. 864) books on the subject of *Ahlâq al-Muluk*.[22] It is clear that he made a synthesis of the Persian and Arabic traditions. The Berlin manuscript has an unequalled chapter titled *The King's Study of the History of the Past Kings and of Other Sciences* (Nazar al-Malik fi al-Siyasa wa ghayriha min al-'ulum). Here the kind of books that should be read by the king are outlined; also, there are notes on how he should read and how should the director (*Sahib*) of the palace library, which he calls Bayt al-Hikma, serve the king.[23] This detailed account relates the fascinating protocol procedures, indicating how the director (*Sahib*) of the palace library should submit the book to the king and repeatedly advises that no one, including the members of his own family, should have information about the kind of books, even a verse of the Qur'an, read by the king. The detailed account on matters relating to the way a book ought to be prepared and submitted to the King are meticulously depicted. This chapter, unlike the others, does not include the name of any Persian or Arab kings that the author refers elsewhere.[24] He does not quote here any specific historical account or anecdote as he frequently does in the rest of the book where he narrates events related to some of the Sassanian kings and Arab caliphs starting from Mu'awiyya, the founder of the Umayyad dynasty to the tenth Abbasid Caliph al-Wathiq (r. 842–848).

The author's repetitive, detailed account of the secrecy and discretion about the king's reading and his prudence in discussing matters related to religion and philosophical matters in his court might be better understood in light of what al-Ma'mun created with his open and straightforward style by pursuing his intellectual interests and siding with the viewpoint of the Mu'tazila on the issue of the Quran's createdness. As the text of this chapter does not lend itself to any exclusive "Persian" context and the author does not refer to the origin of the term Bayt al-Hikma as an appellation for the royal library, it is hard to sustain that this institute was mainly of Persian origin and the name was the translation of its unmentioned Persian equivalent. It is evident that the author is using an already established expression.

It could also be inferred that since references to the Abbasid Caliphs do not go beyond al-Wathiq, the predecessor of al-Mutawakkil who abandoned the oppressive policy of al-Ma'mun, it could be argued that this book was written either during the reign of al-Wathiq or shortly after his death, hence the remarks concerning the secrecy about the books read by the caliph and the discussions held with his courtiers on religious and philosophical subjects. This must be a reaction to the great controversy and his disapproval of al-Ma'mun's frank and open approach to such matters. It is more sensible to consider that this secrecy and prudence is more in line with the growing opposition to the mihna (ordeal) created by al-Ma'mun and abandoned around 850 by al-Wathiq's successor al-Mutawakkil.

Notes

1 Quated by Jawad Ali, "Mawarid ta'rikh al-Tabari", Majallat al-Maj'ma al-Ilmi al-Iraqi, Vol. 2, 1951, pp. 142, 143.
2 Abu Ishaq Ibrahim bin Ali al-Husayn al-Qayrewani, *Zeyl Zahr el-Adab*, edited by Mohammed Ali al-Bijawi, Cairo, Vol. 1, pp. 77, 78.
3 Al-Muqaddisi, *The Best Divisions of Knowledge of the Regions, Ahsan al-Taqasim fi Marifat al-Aqalim*, Garnet Publishing, 2000, p. 395. (Quoted by Amira K. Bennison, *The Great Caliph: The Golden Age of the Abbasid Empire*, Tauris, 2009, p. 180.)
4 William Gohlman, *The Life of Ibn Sina: A Critical Edition and Annotated Translation*, Albany State University of New York Press, 1974, pp. 36, 37.
5 Katip Çelebi, *Kashf al-Zunun*, edited by E. Ihsanoglu, B.A. Marouf, London, al-Furqan Foundation, 2021, Vol. 3, p. 412.
6 See Ibn Juljul, 1955, p. 65; Ibn Al-Qifti, 1903, p. 380; Ibn Abi Usaybia, 1965, p. 246.
7 For questioning Ibn Juljul above mentioned account see comments of Fuad Sayid in page 65 about the non-matching dates of the conquest of these places with Abbasid reign. It is also clear that the dates of the conquest of these places do not correspond to what mentioned in the narrative.
8 AN II, pp. 143–147; for English translation see, Dodge, p. 584.
9 Ibn Nubate al-Masri, *Sarh al-'uyun fi Qasidat Ibn Zaydun*, edited by Abu al-Fadl Ibrahim, Cairo, 1964, p. 242.
10 This story was reported by al-Khatib al-Baghdadi, al-Hafedh Abubakr Ahmed, *The History of Baghdad or The City of Peace*, Cairo, 1931, Vol. 14, pp. 149, 150; Yaqut al-Hamawi, *Mu'jam al-Udaba*, Vol. 19, Cairo, Dar al-Ma'mun, pp. 11, 12; Ibn Khalkan, Shamsuddin Abu al-Abbas, *Wafiyatul A'yan Wa Anba' Abna'u Zaman*, edited by Ihsan Abbas, Beirut, 1969, Vol. 6, p. 177. The period over which Ibn al-Farra authored the book al-Hudud is said to be "several years" in al-Baghdadi's report, whereas Ibn Khalkan sets it at "two years" and it is the latter that we have considered as most likely.

What Was the Reality? 67

11 In classic Arabic "Dar" means a house, mansion house of large size, comprising a court or a house comprising several sets of apartments and a court, a place of abode which comprises a building or buildings and court. See E.W. Lane, p. 931.
12 For example, see Abd al-Jabbar Naji, *Bayt al-Hikma al Baghdadi*, Baghdad, 2008, pp. 8, 59.
13 D. Gutas, pp. 54, 59
14 AN I, p. 327; B. Dodge, p. 639.
15 AN II, pp. 141–143; B. Dodge, pp. 583, 584.
16 Ibid.
17 D. Gutas, p. 54.
18 AN I, p. 134.
19 There are unjustified claims to this end in some newly published studies. See the strange lists in Attallah's book, pp. 258–320.
20 Al-Qifti, pp. 171–177.
21 For a discussion of the book and its author and its relation to similar literature, see F. Rosenthal, "From Arabic Books and Manuscripts, XVI: As-Sarakhsi (?) on the Appropriate Behavior for Kings", *Journal of the American Oriental Society*, Vol. 115, 1995, pp. 105–109.

Also see Mohammed-Taqi Danishpazhouh, *An annotated Bibliography on Government and Statecraft in Authority and Political Culture in Shi'ism*, edited by S.A. Argomaud, Suny Press, 1988.
22 The author in his introduction writes this name as Haris al-Ta'ǧlibi; however, in the rest of his book, he mentioned the correct name of Haris al-Tha'labi.
23 Berlin, Mss. Or. Oct. 2673 (copied on 630/1232). Abu'l Hasan Ali bin Razin, Adab al-Muluk, Beirut, Dar al-Tali'a wa al-nashr, 2001; based on this unique manuscript the text has been edited and published by Jalil al-Atiyya.
24 Abul'l-Hasan 'Âli b. Razin, Kitabu Adab al-Muluk, Berlin Manuscript or. oct. 2673, ff.9a–14b; the published edition pp. 45–49

Part VIII What Happened to the House of Wisdom?

At this point of our assessment of the functioning of the House of Wisdom, it became obvious that there was only one institute in the Abbasid Caliph's palace but which acquired two names. The first name was a straightforward depiction as a library to be mentioned with its founder or promoter's name. The second name was an attribution to its collection of books related to the pre-Islamic knowledge of sciences (ulum al-awa'il) and philosophy (hikma) and becoming associated with a philosophically motivated school of thought. Thus, its depiction as the House of Wisdom became an established compound name.

To address the question raised in the title of this part of the book, it is imperative to answer another basic question: What was the relation of the House of Wisdom with the Inquisition (Mihna)?

To speak about the relation between the *Mihna* and the House of Wisdom cannot be sustained from the accounts mentioned in the primary sources. Abu al-Fida (d. 1331), a prominent historian from the Mamluk era, narrates that al-Ma'mun in 212/827 went public with his opinion on the createdness of the Qur'an. Eche endorses Abu al-Fida's statement and contextualizes it with another Mamluk historian Ibn Taghribirdi's statement that "al-Ma'mun brought closer the theologians and ordered them to debate in his presence". Eche interpreted this statement freely with alteration to its meaning by saying that al-Ma'mun installed them in the House of Wisdom.[1] This public disclosure of al-Ma'mun took place three years after the alleged "installation" of *mutakallimun* (philosophical theologians) at the House of Wisdom. Meanwhile, the *Mihna* occurred in 218/833, five years after the caliph's declaration of his sponsorship and nine years after the said installation of *mutakallimun* in the House of Wisdom. In reference to scholarly meetings and discussions in the presence of the caliph at the House of Wisdom, the account of the debate between Abd al-Aziz

What Happened to the House of Wisdom? 69

al-Kinani and Bishr al-Marisi is quoted by Eche as an example par excellence for association of House of Wisdom with this debate, which we have already shown was not correct (see Part VI).

The policy of inquisition continued in the reign of al-Wathiq (d. 842/471) then the first three years of al-Mutawakkil (r. 847–861) when it was abandoned. Primary sources do not have clues to what was the fate of the House of Wisdom all these years. However, modern studies speak about the closure and the reopening of the House of Wisdom. Meyerhof says that it was "reopened" during the reign of al-Mutawakkil.[2] De Lacy O'Leary in his study on how Greek science passed to Islam, in an unqualified and strange statement, states that al-Mutawakkil was of sadistic temperament, mischievous, and capriciously cruel. Though not himself a scholar like al-Ma'mun, he was a patron of science and scholarship and reopened the House of Wisdom, granting it fresh endowments (!). He also observes that the best work of translation was done during his reign as the training of the stuff and experience were bearing fruits.[3] D. Sourdel casts doubt on the fate of the House of Wisdom after al-Mutawakkil stopped the inquisition and she maintains that the House of Wisdom does not appear to have survived the orthodox reaction.[4]

What we can gather from the statement of Ibn Taghribirdi is that besides al-Ma'mun's well-known involvement and support to the issue of the createdness of the Qur'an and favoring their proponents, those who supported his views made use of his palace library where it held numerous books on Hikma/Wisdom, and furthermore that he supported them financially. Hence this library became known as Bayt al-Hikma/House of Wisdom because of its collection of books on Hikma/Wisdom and for being a place where they had philosophic deliberations and disputations. Between the death of al-Ma'mun in 833, four months after his declaration of the inquisition, and Mutawakkil's abandoning the inquisition in 850, we can expect that the involvement of the royal library with such activities did not last long. Meanwhile, we have no information about what happened to the House of Wisdom and its relationship with the supporters of the inquisition. Nevertheless, since the capital of the Abbasid caliphate was moved from Baghdad to the newly established city of Samarra 125 km north of Baghdad three years after the death of al-Ma'mun, it is safe to conclude that "the House of Wisdom" lost its glamor and became known as the library of al-Ma'mun. So, it became known as other libraries have with its name attributed to its founder. We have many accounts from the tenth century that show that scholars had access to this library collection. Hamza al-Isfahani (d. 360/970) mentions in the introduction of his history book that he had access to a copy from Khizanat al-Ma'mun (library of al-Ma'mun).[5]

As already explained in Part III, Al-Nadim's *Fihrist* provides ample and clear evidence for the change in the qualifications of the palace library. So, when he speaks about the palace library during the reign of Harun al-Rashid and al-Ma'mun, he refers to it as Khizanat al-Hikma (the repository of Wisdom) or Bayt al-Hikma (the House of Wisdom).[6] When he mentions his personal experience with this library one and a half centuries after the death of al-Ma'mun, he says simply Khizanat al-Ma'mun (the repository of al-Ma'mun).[7]

The same al-Nadim, when speaking about the same institution during the reign of Harun al-Rashid and al-Ma'mun, qualifies the repository as the library of wisdom of Harun al-Rashid[8] and the same for al-Ma'mun, respectively.[9]

These accounts of al-Nadim clearly showed that the library was there, and that scholars could consult its collections.[10]

The famous biographer Ibn Abi Usaybi'a (d. 633/1245) in his biography of Hunayn Ibn Ishaq tells us that he has seen a number of Galen's books and other books carrying remarks written in the Greek language by Hunayn Ibn Ishaq and carrying the sign of al-Ma'mun's [library].[11] Ibn Abi Usaybi'a does not clarify where he had access to these books. Was that in Baghdad at what remained of the library of al-Ma'mun, or had these books found their way to the book market? Al-Nadim in a previous quotation tells us that he "has seen certain books in the library of al-Ma'mun" or he has copied certain parts from books existing in the library of al-Ma'mun.[12] In one place he says that he had got an old copy of a book that seems to belong to al-Ma'mun's library.[13] When this account is read with the account of Ibn Abi Usaybi'a who spent his life in Damascus and Cairo and did not live in Baghdad, we can understand that the books belonging to this royal library found their way out into the hands of bibliophiles up to the thirteenth century.

The date of Ibn Abi Usaybi'a's death was one decade before the sack of Baghdad by Ilkhanate Mongol forces (656/1258). Al-Qalqashandi (d. 1418) narrates in his encyclopedic work Subh al-'Asha, in an account on famous libraries in Islam, that the library (khizana) of the Abbasid Caliphs in Baghdad was one of the most magnificent ones and that it survived until the Mongols sacked Baghdad and killed the Caliph al-Musta'sim (r. 1248–1258) and that "the library has gone among other things, its signs were lost and its remains were erased".[14]

After this brief account of al-Qalqashandi, we can come back to our own assessment. The claim of the closure and reopening of the

What Happened to the House of Wisdom? 71

House of Wisdom comes from a basic assumption that there was an independent institution with this name and since it was associated with the Mu'tazilas and the inquisition, so too must it have been a target of the anti-Mu'tazile policy. However, it is clear from the different examples given above that this was not the case and that this specific appellation of the House of Wisdom given to the Abbasid palace library was subsequently abandoned. We can conclude further that the library was maintained under the name of library of al-Ma'mun. The account of al-Qalqashandi shows that this library survived until the invasion of Baghdad by the Mongols.

The assumption that there was a closure date of the House of Wisdom is as baseless as the claim of its establishment date of 830 (see Part II). So, fixing a date of closure for House of Wisdom in the time of al-Mutawakkil has no historic evidence, any more than the date of its establishment during the reign of al-Ma'mun.

To answer the question raised in the title of this part of the book, what happened to the House of Wisdom after the death of al-Ma'mun? The answer is very simple and straight forward: nothing, since there was no independent and separate institution with the appellation of the House of Wisdom. The library that acquired this appellation because of its collection of books and for being a place for deliberation and philosophical discussions faced the same destiny as other large libraries.

Notes

1 Y. Eche, pp. 53, 54.
2 M. Meyerhof, Alexandria, p. 403.
3 De Lacy O'Leary, *How Greek Science Passed to the Arabs*, Goodword Books, 2002, p. 168. This is the first time there is a mention to the House of Wisdom that was granted a fresh endowment as if there was an "old endowment".
4 Dominique Sourdel, EI^2; Also see this book Part V, footnote 24.
5 J.M.E. Gottwaldt, pp. 8, 9.
6 AN I, pp. 25, 373, 374; AN II, 142, 235, 326.
7 AN I, pp. 13, 14, 44, 51.
8 AN II, p. 234; Dodge, p. 651.
9 AN II, p. 235; Dodge, p. 652; see also, AN I, 24; Dodge, p. 18.
10 AN I, pp. 13, 14, 44, 51.
11 Ibn Abi Usaybi'a, p. 260.
12 AN I, pp. 13, 14, 44.
13 AN I, p. 51.
14 Al-Qalqashandi, *Subh al-Asha*, Dar al Kutub, Cairo, 1963, Vol. I, p. 466.

Part IX The Impact

The Abbasid palace library that flourished under the reigns of Harun al-Rashid and al-Ma'mun and became known as the House of Wisdom inspired scholars and intellectuals belonging to the retinue of the caliphs to emulate their master and establish similar libraries. By the end of the eighth century acquiring books was easier and cheaper due to the introduction of paper manufacturing in Baghdad after the Battle of Talas (134/751). The Fatimid institute of learning with the similar name of Dar al-Hikma (The House of Wisdom), which was established in Cairo almost two centuries after the Abbasid one, has been claimed to be a continuation of al-Ma'mun's House of Wisdom, despite the nonexistence of historical evidence.[1]

Two prominent figures, who served long tenures in the Abbasid Court and were associated with Caliph al-Muwakkil, established their own libraries. The first one was Ali b. Yahya al-Munajjim (d. 275/888) son of Yahya b. Abi Mansur who was an astrologer working for al-Ma'mun.[2] Ali b. Yahya al-Munajjim was one of the first Abbasid intellectuals to build a library which he called *"Khizanat al-Hikma"* located in his residence in the vicinity of Baghdad and which was open to all scholars and visitors. Ali b. Yahya al-Munajjim was also one of the clients of the great Nestorian translators of the Greek works on philosophy and medicine, Hunayn Ibn Ishaq (d. 260/873) and his son Ishaq b. Hunayn (d. 298/910).[3]

The second prominent figure was Fath Ibn Haqan (d. 244/861) a descendent of a Turkish royal family.[4] He was very close to the Caliph al-Mutawakkil and one of the most famous bibliophiles ever heard of in history. We are even told that he always carried a book with him, hidden under his sleeve, and whenever and wherever he found the slightest occasion, he pulled it out from his sleeve and started reading.[5] He himself was an author and poet (in Arabic) and patron of many prominent Arab authors and poets including al-Jahiz and al-Buhteri. His library is referred as *Khizanat al-Hikma*. Ali bin Yahya al-Munajjim was put in charge of building the collection of this library and he transferred a great number of books there that were part of his own collection, as well as books that he had had copied for Fath Ibn Haqan. We are told that this was the biggest and most organized library ever seen.[6]

A third example to mention in this context is the library of the three sons of Musa bin Shakir known as the Banu al-Munajjim (sons of astrologer/astronomer): Muhammad, Ahmad, and al-Hasan. They were avid collectors of books on the classical sciences, mainly geometry, applied mechanics, music, and astrology.[7] Following al-Ma'mun's tradition, we are told that they even sent Hunayn Ibn Ishaq to Byzantium to gather works in the disciplines mentioned above and that the latter returned with rare and strange books in the fields of philosophy, geometry, music, arithmetic, and medicine. They also employed translators such as Hunayn Ibn Ishaq, Hubaysh Ibn al-Hasan, Thabit Ibn Qurra, and others to copy and translate, and that they were spending 500 dinars a month for copying, translating, and attendance (mulazama).[8]

These friends of the arts and sciences had close relations with one another and with the Caliphs al-Ma'mun and al-Mutawakkil.[9] In their *Khizanat al-Hikma*, on a more modest and private scale, they followed the methods and goals pursued by the caliphs in the *Bayt al-Hikma*.[10] The *'ulum al-'awa'il* were among the sciences promoted and pursued in these libraries and this continued even after al-Mutawakkil put an end to the *mihna*. Significantly enough, the existence of private libraries patterned on the institution of *Bayt al-Hikma* confirms the fact that although al-Mutawakkil reduced the role of the Mu'tazilis and brought their political power to a halt, he was not "reacting" against the sciences they promoted.

The following account by Yaqut al-Hamawi (d. 1229) sheds light on the functioning of such private libraries.[11] He narrates that this great library was placed in the magnificent palace of Ali bin Yahya al-Munajjim and that he used to call his library Khizanat al-Hikma, that is to say the Repository of Wisdom. We are also told that it was open for people from all over and contained rooms where they could stay, access the books, and study different disciplines, and that they were taken care of by the host. Yaqut narrates the story of the astrologer Abu Ma'shar (766–886) who was on his way to the pilgrimage. Abu Ma'shar, having limited knowledge about the stars at the time, and after hearing of the fame of this library he decided to visit it and he was astonished with the magnificent library and he decided to stay on there, to study and abandon his travel to pilgrimage. He was deeply engaged until he became an atheist and that was his last interest with religion and Islam.[12]

These private libraries that were patterned on the *Bayt al-Hikma* (without the latter's political ulterior motives), and called its emulators by Y. Eche, would have never come into existence had the Abbasid caliphs, and in particular al-Mutawakkil, been opposed to the sciences studied there. The three "emulator" libraries described above, with the exception of the last one, which was simply referred to as the Banu'l-Munajjim's library, included the word *"hikma"* in their name: *Khizanat al-Hikma*. Later, the term *"hikma"* is replaced by the word *"ilm"* (knowledge/science) and private libraries are called *"Dar al-'Ilm"*. We assume that this change in the nomenclature is the result of a transformation in the cultural paradigms and certain sensitivity towards the use of the term *"hikma"* which was often associated with the Mu'tazila doctrine, Ismaili sect, or other dissenting doctrines considered heterodox and marginal to Sunni Islam.

The inquisition policy and the persecution of the opponents of the createdness of the Qur'an continued during the reigns of four Caliphs al-Ma'mun, al-Mu'tasım, al-Wathiq, and first years of al-Mutawakkil's reign. The struggle against this policy was led by Ahmad Ibn Hanbal (d. 241/855) and come to an end by the decision of al-Mutwakkil in 850. Thus, the supremacy of the Mu'tazilites ended and their political power never recovered.

Private libraries dedicated to the sciences of the ancients continued and engagement with these sciences carried on. Meanwhile, as Prof. Gutas has shown in detail, the inquisition did not affect the translation movement directly or immediately, for it continued to flourish for the rest of the ninth century and throughout the tenth century.[13]

In the pre-inquisition Abbasid society, there was no such conflict or struggle between different schools of thought. However, the struggle between the proponents and opponents of the createdness of the Qur'an led to the emergence of a sensitivity and polarization among the followers of the two parties. The inquisition galvanized the emergence of the *ulema* as a real force and cohesive community within Islamic society. It also paved the way for their political role as a pressure group. The abandonment of the inquisition was tantamount to making the Sunni form of Islam the official religion of the caliphate and giving the *ulema* an assured place in it.[14]

Western scholars like Goldziher (d. 1921) and G. Makdisi (d. 2002) portrayed this struggle as a fight between rivals and a dichotomy that lasted forever. Aydın Sayılı (d. 1993), in his PhD dissertation on the history of institutions of learning in Islam, quoted Goldziher's key sentence: "Muslim theologians, therefore, come to consider as desirable only those branches of learning which had grown directly of their religion. Sciences which owed their origin to foreign sources were regarded at least with suspicion".[15] Sayılı built his study of the history of institutions of learning in Islam on this premise as well as on the notion of the deliberate exclusion of the ancient sciences from the madrasa teaching programs.

The supposed antiphilosophical attitude of Muslim scholars constituted the intellectual background of the development of madrasa education in Islam. This "epistemological dichotomy" has also been expressed on the institutional level as G. Makdisi proposes in his study on the historical development of the *madrasa* entitled "The Rise of Colleges". He considers that there is a dichotomy in the fields of knowledge and in the institutions of learning in the Islamic world. For Makdisi, there are two sets of antagonistic sciences: the "religious" and the "foreign". These are upheld by two types of learning institutions, the *madrasa*, which he calls "college", exclusively devoted to the teaching of religious sciences, and on the other hand, the private establishments where the study of the secular scientific domains was pursued. The *madrasa* was conceived by Makdisi as an institution devoted only to the teaching of Islamic law, fiqh and the training of jurists, faqihs. He stretches his theory to "exclude" all subjects other than law and its ancillaries. He states, "the dichotomy in the fields of knowledge was matched by a dichotomy in the institutions of learning".[16] When we look at the works of A. Sayılı and Y. Eche that prepared the grounds for Makdisi's definite judgment, we find that these studies were based on fundamentally accepted concepts of "exclusion" and "dichotomy".[17]

Both Eche and Sayılı belonged to the same generation. The Syrian scholar coming to Paris from *de jure* independent Syria was aspiring to the Arab awakening, so he wanted to foresee in his national heritage a fully-fledged modern library and an advanced academy of sciences. Meanwhile, Aydın Sayılı who owed his opportunity to study the history of science in Harvard University to Atatürk, the founder of Republic of Turkey, was a true believer and follower of his reforms.

Sayılı adopted two approaches which he called "methods" where he rationalized his arguments on the basis of his commitment to the contemporary republican Turkish experience of modernization, which was based on the assumption of the decline of Islamic Ottoman civilization as well as on taking the European model as an example. The first of these approaches is the assertion that Islam was essentially a nonplastic and stable society and culture, and many of its features were hardly altered until relatively recent attempts of westernization. The distant past could be studied more directly through the recent past, or even, the present. Different mental attitudes, which are not ascertainable through the extant source material, can be grasped with the help of residual evidence. Also, the reactions to the recent attempts at westernization would be helpful in determining the obstacles to the study of the sciences. Secondly, he maintained that arriving at conclusions through rationalization might also be guided by considering the applicability of the same reasoning to Western Europe, which was also a theocentric society. Sayılı, utilizing these approaches in some cases, concluded his long dissertation on the institutionalization of science and learning, which he wrote under the influence of his mentor G. Sarton's theory of the "Golden Age of Science in Islam" (approximately up to 1000 AD) and the firm belief in the paradigm of the decline of Islamic civilization as it was prevailing in the Turkish republican discourse, by saying:

> In short, in Islam the natural, physical and mathematical sciences derived trivial benefit from the school and from other institutions of science and learning. It is obvious, therefore, that their cultivation had to depend on private instruction i.e., learning from private teachers and by self-instruction.[18]

Through generations of scholars the above-mentioned notions developed by Goldziher, G. Sarton, A. Sayılı, Y. Eche, and G. Makdisi were taken for granted and they have been prevalent. However, recently these notions have begun to be challenged in two aspects. D. Gutas has taken to task the misconception of Goldziher and his assumption that old Islamic orthodoxy was against the sciences of the ancients and has elaborately showed that there was a "rational and even political bias" behind Goldziher's position.[19] The other challenge was raised against the notion of a dichotomy and exclusionist propositions, which was built on a detailed study of different institutions of learning in the Arab, Persian, and Ottoman realms all through the classical age up to the sixteenth century. These studies proposed that there was no dichotomy but integration, no exclusion but gradual inclusion.[20]

Notes

1 For a short introduction to the Fatimid institution and its relation to the Abbasid House of Wisdom, see Part I, endnote 22.
2 For Yahya b. Abi Mansur, AN II, p. 237; Rosenfeld-Ihsanoglu, No. 31.
3 Balty-Gueston, "Le Bayt al-Hikma de Baghdad", p. 145.
4 O. Pinto, "al-Fath b. Khakan", EI², Vol. II, Brill, pp. 837, 838; Hugh Kennedy, *When Baghdad Ruled the Muslim World: The Rise and Fall of Islam's Greatest Dynasty*, Boston, MA: Da Capo Press, 2006. Kennedy calls him "the greatest bibliophile of his day".
5 Ibn Khalliqan, *Wafayat al-'A'yan wa 'Anba' 'Abna' al-Zaman*, edited by Ihsan Abbas, Vol. 6, Beirut, n.d., pp. 176–178; see also O. Pinto, "al-Fath b. Khakan", EI², p. 837; D. Sourdel, *Le Vizarat Abbaside*, Damas, 1959, pp. 282–286.
6 AN I, pp. 261, 362, 442, 457; Ibn Khalliqan, *Wafayat*, p. 56; Yaqut, *Mu'jam al-Udaba*, Vol. 15, p. 157.
7 AN II, pp. 224–226; al-Qifti, pp. 441–443.
8 AN I, p. 361; al-Qifti, pp. 30, 31.
9 Y. Eche, *Les Bibliotheques Arabes*, p. 41.
10 Ibid., p. 63.
11 Yaqut al-Hamawi, p. 157.
12 AN II, p. 242; also see Rosenfeld-Ihsanoglu, No. 88.
13 D. Gutas, pp. 151–165.
14 Watt, p. 42.
15 I. Goldziher, "Stellung der alten islamischen Orthodoxie zu den antiken Wissenschaften", *Abhandlungen der Königlich Preussischen Akademie der Wissenschaften*, Jahrgang 1915, Philosophisch-historische Klasse, No. 8, Berlin, Verlag der Akademie, 1916, quoted by Sayılı dissertation p. 47.
16 George Makdisi, *The Rise of College*, p. 78.
17 Aydın Sayılı, "The Institutions of Science and Learning in the Muslim World", Ph.D. Thesis, Harvard University, Department of the History of Science and Learning, 1941; Youssef Eche, *Les bibliothèques arabes publiques et semi-publiques en Mésopotamie, en Syrie et en Égypte au Moyen Age*, Damascus, Institute Français de Damas, 1967.
18 Sayılı, "The Institutions of Science...", p. 35.
19 Gutas, pp. 166–175.
20 Our study on these issues has been in progress for long time, see Ihsanoglu, "Institutions of Science Education", pp. 386–397; Ihsanoglu, Il Ruolo Delle Istituzioni, pp. 110–139; "Institutionalization of Science in the Medreses of Pre-Ottoman and Ottoman Turkey Institutions", in *Turkish Studies in the History and Philosophy of Science. Boston Studies in the Philosophy of Science*, Vol. 244, edited by Irzik G., Güzeldere G., Dordrecht, Springer, 2005; also published in Ihsanoglu, Studies on Ottoman Science and Culture, Variorum Routledge, 2019, p. 69.

Part X Concluding Remarks

The main difficulty in comprehending the nature of the Abbasid palace library, at times referred to as "Khizanat al-Hikma" (Repository of Wisdom) and at others as "Bayt al-Hikma" (House of Wisdom) is how to situate this library within the overall framework of the multifaceted cultural activities in the era of both of the Caliphs Harun al-Rashid and al-Ma'mun. What is certain about these activities is that they were, in the main, held under the caliphal patronage. Indeed, the poets, the literary figures, religious scholars, physicians, astronomers, and astrologers who belonged to different religions and hailed from varied origins, exercised their activities under the patronage of the caliph and with his financial support. Naturally, there was a larger scope of patronage based at the court. Among the patrons were the caliph's men, wealthy scholars, and the rich people who were interested in various elements of cultural activities.

It is obvious that Bayt al-Hikma was administered by a director called "sahib Bayt al-Hikma". Al-Nadim confirms this and gives the names of Salam in Harun al-Rashid and Sahl bin Harun who undertook this post during al-Ma'mun's reign. From al-Nadim's *Fihrist* and other biographical sources, it could easily be maintained that the functions of the director (sahib) were more than a librarian, and his functions were not limited to collecting, copying, and preserving the books, but included translating and supervising the translation of books to Arabic.

Again, it is al-Nadim who says that there were scholars working at this institution during the reigns of these two caliphs. He reports that Abu Sahl Ibn Nawbakht was one of the functionaries at Harun al-Rashid's Khizanat al-Hikma and made translations from Persian. Al-Qifti also says that al-Fadl Ibn Nawbakht was entrusted with the administration of the Khizanat. According to al-Nadim, the famous mathematician, astronomer, and geographer Muhammad b. Musa al-Khawarazmi, who dedicated some of his works to al-Ma'mun, devoted himself and his time to "Khizanat al-Hikma of al- Ma'mun". The term "munqati" used here by al-Nadim and other examples indicate the different types of association of the scholars with the Bayt al-Hikma. Again, we are also informed that the gifted three sons of astronomer Musa bin Shakir were placed under the supervision of Yahya Ibn Mansur at Bayt al-Hikma. This report demonstrates that there were scholars who were permanently working at Bayt al-Hikma and some sort of private education was pursued.

Notwithstanding all these, the attempt to reconstruct or draw a complete picture of Bayt al-Hikma is a rather difficult task due to the unavailability of any detailed historical accounts related to this institution. The speculation made by early scholars who wrote on the subject, as well as the carelessness of some of them have created an unrealistic, anachronistic, and inflamed image of Bayt al-Hikma. Nevertheless, the historical reality should not be prevaricated, and different notions related to this institution should not be ignored.

Meanwhile, as much as taking a modern "maximalist" approach to the subject by construing this institution as a full-fledged "academy" and drawing an exaggerated picture that is contradictory to the historical facts is wrong; the "minimalist" approach thinking of this institution solely as a library where exclusively translations from Persian were made, would be also ignoring the historical records completely. According to the information given by al-Asma'i, al-Jahiz, and al-Nadim, Bayt al-Hikma was an institution where compilations and translations from Persian and Greek were made.

This study showed that generations of scholars addressing the history of the House of Wisdom overlooked historical context and they were reading about modern institutions in classical texts, idealizing their structure, and functioning in a way that reflected their own ambitions.

As a matter of fact, the concept of an academy structured around the European model or modern university as referred to in Part II of this book is anachronistic and inadmissible, and any discussion to that end would be meaningless.

This study has dismissed many claims and propositions that were generated and continued by generations of scholars, and which became a priori self-evident propositions. It also showed that elitist institutions in the absence of proper funding would lose their sustainability if they did not care for the sensitivities of the public and if they harbored the heterodox interests.

80 Concluding Remarks

There are, to all evidence, certain specific figures as mentioned in the primary sources who were attached to the palace library and who did work there officially. They are quite limited in numbers, but they stand as a proof to the existence of some mode of institutional, organized work within the palace library that goes beyond the mere collection and preservation of books and encompasses other activities such as authoring, translating, and copying books.

As for depicting al-Nadim's book *al-Fihrist*, which offers real chronicles of the cultural activities and constitutes a record of what al-Nadim witnessed in terms of authorship and translation activities in the first Abbasid era, as a catalogue of the House of Wisdom or claiming that all the scholars, literary figures, translators, astronomers, astrologers, and physicians who lived and practiced during that era used to write or translate books as official employees at this sort of "academy" that would have had well-defined programs and specific budgets similar to what we have today, it simply does not coincide with the available historical narratives and is certainly anachronistic.

The myths surrounding the House of Wisdom can no longer stand in the face of reality.

Bibliography

Reference Works

Brockelmann, Carl, *Geschichte der arabischen Literatur*, Vol. I, Weimar, Emil Felber Verlag, 1898.
Brockelmann, Carl, *Geschichte der arabischen Litteratur*, Vol. I, Leiden, E.J. Brill, 1937.
Encyclopedia of Islam, 2nd Edition, Leiden, Brill, 1960–2002.
Encyclopedia of Islam, 3rd Edition, Leiden, Brill, 2007–.
Lane, Edward William, *Arabic-English Lexicon*, The Islamic Texts Society; New Edition Vol. I–II, 1984.
Liddel, Henry George and Schott Robert, *A Greek-English Lexicon*, Oxford, Clarendon Press, 1968.
Rosenfeld, Boris A. and Ekmeleddin İhsanoğlu, *Mathematicians, Astronomers, and Other Scholars of Islamic Civilization and Their Works (7th–19th c.)*, İstanbul, IRCICA, 2003.
Sarton, George, *Introduction to the History of Science*, Vol. I, Huntingdon, NY, Krieger, 1975.
Steingass, Francis Joseph, *Persian – English Dictionary*, 6th Edition, London, Routledge, 1977.
Suter, Heinrich, *Die Mathematiker und Astronomen der Araber und ihre Werke, Abhandle zur Geschichte den Wisseneschaften Heft*, Leipzig, B.G. Teubner, 1900.
Ulmann, Manfred, *Wörterbuch Zu den Grichisch-Arabischen Übersetzungen des 9. Jahrhunderts*, Harrowitz Verlag, Wiesbaden, 2002.

Primary Sources

Abu al-Faradj al-Isfahani, *Al-Aghani*, Vol. 4, Cairo, Wizarat al-Thaqafa wa al-Irshad al Qawmi, n.d.
Abu Ishaq Ibrahim bin Ali al-Husari al-Qayrewani, *Zeyl Zahr el-Adab*, Vol. 1., Cairo, al-Mektebe al-tijariyya al-kubra, n.d.
Abu'l Hasan Ali bin Razin, *Adab al-Muluk*, edited by Jalil al-Atiyya, Beirut, Dar al-Tali'a wa al-nashr, 2001.

Bibliography

Al-Balazuri, *Kitab Jumal min Ansab al-Ashraf*, edited by Suhayl Zakkar, Riyad Zirikli, Vol. 6, Beirut, Dar al-Fikr, 1996.

Al-Darimi, *Rad al-Imam al-Darimi 'Osman b. Sa'id 'ala Bash al-Marisi al 'Anid*, edited by Muhammad Hamid al-Faqi, Beirut, Dar al-Kutub al-'Ilmiyya, n.d.

Al-Isfahani, Hamza, *Kitab al-Amthal al-Sadira 'an Buyut al-shi'r*, Berlin manuscript, or. quart. n. 1215, ff.1a-6b.

Al-Khatib al-Baghdadi, *al-Hafedh Abubakr Ahmed (d. 463/1070): the history of Baghdad or the City of Peace*, Cairo, Vol. 14, 1931.

Al-Kinani, Abd al-Aziz bin Yahya, *Kitab al-Hayda*, edited by Jamil Saliba, Damascus, Arab Academy, 1964.

Al-Kinani, Abd al-Aziz bin Yahya, *Kitab al-Hayda*, Zahiriyye Manuscript Collection, Damascus, Tassawuf No, 129, f.67-b.

Al-Masudi, *Muruj al-Zahab*, Cairo, 1249 (2/27).

Al-Masudi, *The Meadows of Gold*, trans. and ed. Paul Lunde and Caroline Stone, London, Kegan Paul, 1989.

Al-Muqaddisi, *The Best Divisions of Knowledge of the Regions*, Ahsan al-Taqasim fi Marifat al-Aqalim, Garnet Publishing, 2000.

Al-Nadim, Abu al-Faraj Muhammed Ibn Ishaq, *The Fihrist*, edited by Ayman Fu'ad Sayyid, Vol. 1–2, London, Al-Furqan Islamic Heritage Foundation, 2014.

Al-Qalqashandi, *Subh al-Asha*, Vol. I, Cairo, Dar al Kutub, 1963.

Al-Qifti, 'Ali ibn Yusuf', *Tarih al-Hukama*, edited by Julius Lippert, Lepzig, Dieterich'sche Verlagsbuchhandlung, 1903.

Bennison, Amira K., *The Great Caliph: The Golden Age of the Abbasid Empire*, London, Tauris, 2009.

Burton, Richard F., A plain and literal translation of the Arabian Nights entertainments now entitled *The Book of the Thousand Nights and a Night*, with introduction explanatory notes on the manners and customs of Moslem men and a terminal essay upon the history of the Nights, edited by Richard F. Burton, Vol. 1, Benares, Kamashastra Society, 1885–1886.

Dodge, Bayard, *The Fihrist of Al-Nadim: A Tenth-Century Survey of Muslim Culture*, Vol. 1–2, Columbia University Press, 1970.

Gottwaldt, Joseph M. E., *Hamzae Ispahanensis*, Annalium, Libri X, Lipsiae, 1848.

Hunayn Ibn Ishaq, Über Die Syrischen und Arabischen Galen-übersetzungen, *zum Ersten Mal Herausgegeben und uberstat von G. Bergstrasser*, Leipzig, 1925.

Ibn Abi Usaybia, *Uyun al-enba' fi tabaqat al- atibba'*, edited by Nizar Rıza, Beirut, Mektebet al-Hayat, n.d.

Ibn al-Ibri, *Tarikh Mukhtasar al-Duwal*, Beirut, n.d.

Ibn al-Subki, *Tabaqat al-Shafiyye al-Kubra*, edited by Abd al-Fettah M. al-Hulu and Mahmud M. al-Tanahi, Vol.2, Cairo, İ. al-Bab al-Halebi, 1964.

Ibn Asakir, *Tarikh Madinat Dimashq*, Vol. 52, edited by Omar Ibn Gharamah al-'Amrawi, Beirut, Dar al-Fikr, 1997.

Ibn Juljul al-Andalusi, Abu Dawud Suleiman Ibn Hassan, *Les Genererations Medecins et Des Sages (Tabaqat al-'Atibba wal-hukamâ')*, edited by Fu'ad Sayyid, Beirut, 1985.
Ibn Hazm al-Andalusi, *Djamharat Ansab al-Arab*, edited by ́Abd al-Salam Mohammad Harun, 5th Edition, Cairo, Dar al-Maarif, 1982.
Ibn Hazm al-Andalusi, *Djamharat Ansab al-Arab*, edited by Levi Provençal, Cairo, Dar al-Maarif, 1948.
Ibn Hawqal, *Suret al-Ard (The face of the Earth)*, 2nd Edition, Vol. I, Leiden, 1938.
Ibn Nubate al-Masri, *Sarh al-'uyun fi Qasidat Ibn Zaydun*, edited by Abu al-Fadl Ibrahim, Cairo, 1964.
Ibn Tahgribirdi, *al-Nujum al-zahira fi muluk Misr wa-l-Qahira*, Vol. 2, Cairo, Dar al-Kulub al-Mısırriyye, 1950.
Katip Çelebi, *Kashf al-Zunun 'An Asami Al-Kutub Wa al-Funûn*, edited by E. Ihsanoglu and B. A. Marouf, London, Al-Furqan Islamic Heritage Foundation, Vol. 3, 2021.
Katib Jelebi, a Mustafa ben Abdallah, *Lexicon bibliographicum et encyclopædicum: ad codicum Vindobonensium Parisiensium et Berolinensis*, edited by Gustavus Fluegel, Tomus septimus, London, 1858. Printed for the Oriental Translation Fund of Great Britain and Ireland
Sa'id al-Andalusi, *Science in the Medieval World, "Book of Categories on Nations"*, trans. and edited by Semaan I. Salem and Alok Kumar, Austin, University of Texas Press, 1991.
Yaqut Al-Hamawi, *Mu'jam al-Udaba*, Vols. 15 and 19, Cairo, Dar al-Ma'mun, n.d.

Secondary Sources

Ali, Jawad, "Mawarid ta'rikh al-Tabari", *Majallat al-Maj'ma al-Ilmi al-Iraqi*, Vol. 2, 1951, pp. 142–143.
Al-Khalili, Jim, *The House of Wisdom*, London, Penguin Books, 2010.
Al-Khatib, al-Baghdadi, al-Hafedh Abubakr Ahmed, *The History of Baghdad or The City of Peace*, Vol. 14, Beirut, Dar al-kitab al-Arabi, n.d.
Attallah, Khedr Ahmed, *Bayt al-Hikma fi 'Asr al-'Abbasyyin*, Cairo, Dar Al Fikr Al-Araby, n.d.
Balty-Gueston, Marie Genevieve, "Bayt al-Hikmah et Politique Culturelle du Calife al-Ma'mun", *Journal of History of Medicine, Medicina Nei Secoli Arte E Scienza*, Vol. 6, 1994, pp. 275–291.
Balty-Gueston, Marie Genevieve, "Le Bayt al-Hikm de Baghdad", *Arabica Journal*, Vol. 39, 1992, pp. 131–150.
Beeston, Alfred Felix Landon, "The 'Ali Ibn Shah' Preface to Kalilah wa Dimnah", *Oriens Journal*, Vol. VII, 1954, p. 81.
Bladel, Kevin, "Bayt al-Hikma", *Encyclopedia of Islam*, 3rd Edition, Leiden, Brill, 2009.
Brockelmann, Carl, "Kalīla wa Dimna", EI², IV, 1978, pp. 503–506.

Bibliography

Brockelmann, Carl, "Der Islam von seinen Anfängen bis auf die Gegenwart", *Ullsteins Weltgeschichte. Die Entwicklung der Menschheit in Staat und Gessellschaft, in Kultur und Geistesleben vol. III: Geschichte des Orients*, edited by Pflugk-Harttung, Julius von, Berlin, Ullstein Verlag, 1910.

Dachraoui, Farhat, "Contribution a l'Histoire des Fatimides en Ifriqya", *Arabica Journal*, Vol. 8, 1961, pp. 189–203.

Danishpazhouh, Mohammed-Taqi, *An annotated Bibliography on Government and Statecraft in Authority and Political Culture in Shi'ism*, edited by S.A. Argomaud, Albany, State University of New York Press, 1988.

De Sacy, Silvestre, *Calila et Dimna ou Fables De Bidpai*, Paris, De L'imprimerie Royale, 1816.

Demirci, Mustafa, *Beytü'l-Hikme*, İnsan Yayınları, 2016.

Eche, Youssef, *Les bibliothèques arabes publiques et semi-publiques en Mésopotamie, en Syrie et en Égypte au Moyen Age*, Damascus, Institute Français de Damas, 1967.

El-Ali, Salah Ahmed "The Foundation of Baghdad", *The Islamic City A Colloquium*, edited by A. H. Hourani and S. M. Stern, Oxford, Bruno Cassier Ltd.; Philadephia, University of Pennsylvania Press, 1970.

Enderwitz, Suzanne, "Shu'ubiyya", *Encyclopedia of Islam*, Vol. 9, Leiden, Brill, 1997, pp. 513–514.

Erünsal, İsmail E., *Ortaçağ İslam Dünyasında Kitap ve Kütüphane*, İstanbul, Timaş Yayınları, 2018.

Fück, Johann, *Arabische Kultur und Islam im Mittelalter: ausgewahlte Schriften*, edited by Manfred Fleischhammer, Wiemar, Hermann Böhlaus Nachfolger, 1981.

Gohlman, William, *The Life of Ibn Sina: A Critical Edition and Annotated Translation*, Albany, State University of New York Press, 1974.

Goichon, Anne-Marie, "Hikma", *Encyclopedia of Islam*, 2nd Edition, Leiden, Brill, pp. 377–378.

Gutas, Dimitri, *Greek Thought, Arabic Culture, the Graeco-Arabic Translation Movement in Baghdad and Early Abbasid Society*, London, Routledge, 1998.

Heinz, Halm, *The Fatimids and Their Tradition of Learning*, London, I.B. Tauris, in association with the Institute of Ismaili Studies, 1997.

Hitti, Philip, *History of Arabs*, London, MacMillan, 1937.

Hunain Ibn Ishaq, Adab al-Falasife (Sentences des Philosophers), *Abbreviation par Mohamed Bin Ali Bin Ibrahim*, Edition Critique, note et Introduction par Abdurrahman Badawi, publication de l'Institue de Manuscript Arabes, Kuwait, 1985

Ibn al-Nadim, *Kitab al-Fihrist*, edited by Gustav Flügel, Vol. 2, Leipzig, F.C.W. Vogel, 1871.

Ibn Khalliqan, *Wafayat al-'A'yan wa 'Anba' 'Abna' al-Zaman*, edited by Ihsan Abbas, Vol. 6, Beirut, Dar Sadir, 1977.

Ihsanoglu, Ekmeleddin, "Il Ruolo Delle Istituzioni", *Storia Della Scienza*, Vol. 3, Rome, Instituto Della Enciclopedia Italiana Fondata da Giovanni Treccani, 2002, pp. 110–139.

Bibliography 85

Ihsanoglu, Ekmeleddin, "Institutions of Learning in Islam During the Classical Period (Eighth to Sixteenth Centuries): A Critical Overview," Edebiyattan Tıp Tarihine Uzun İnce Bir Yol: Festschrift in Honor of Nuran Yıldırım II, *Journal of Turkish Studies / Türklük Bilgisi Araştırmaları*, Harvard University, Vol. 56, 2001.

Ihsanoglu, Ekmeleddin, "Institutionalization of Science in the Medreses of Pre-Ottoman and Ottoman Turkey Institutions", *Turkish Studies in the History and Philosophy of Science. Boston Studies in the Philosophy of Science*, edited by Irzik G., Güzeldere G., Vol. 244, Dordrecht, Springer, 2005.

Ihsanoglu, Ekmeleddin, "Institutions of Science Education", in *Oxford Encyclopedia of Philosophy, Science and Technology in Islam*, edited by Ibrahim Kalın, Vol. I, Oxford, Oxford University Press, 2014, pp. 386–397.

Ihsanoglu, Ekmeleddin, *Studies on Ottoman Science and Culture*, Variorum, London, Routledge, 2019.

İsmail bin Ali b. Mahmud b. Muhammed bin Umar b. Shahinshah bin Ayyub, Abulfeda, Géographie D'aboulféda, Kitab Taqwim al-Buldun, M. Reinaud and M. Le bon Mac Guckin de Slane (eds.), Paris, L'imprimerie Royale, 1840.

Kennedy, Hugh, *When Baghdad Ruled the Muslim World: The Rise and Fall of Islam's Greatest Dynasty*, Boston, MA, Da Capo Press, 2006.

Lapidus, Ira M., *A History of Islamic Societies*, 3rd Edition, 2014, 6th print, Cambridge, Cambridge University Press, 2020.

Lapidus, Ira M., *A History of Islamic Societies*, Cambridge, Cambridge University Press, 1993.

Lassner, Jacob, "The Caliph's Personal Domain the City Plan of Baghdad Reexamined", *The Islamic City A Colloquium*, edited by A. H. Hourani and S. M. Stern, published by Bruno Cassiran, Oxford University Press and University of Pennsylvania Press, 1970.

Lewis, Bernard, *The Middle East 2000 years of History*, London, Phoenix Press, 2001.

Lyons, Jonathan, *The House of Wisdom*, Newark, P. Bloomsbury Press, 2009.

Majid b. 'Abbud b. Sa'id Badahdah, "Books and Bookmaking during the Time of Prophet Mohammed (Peace be Upon Him) and Khula fa'al al-Rashideen; Effects and Initiatives", Master's Thesis, King Abdul Aziz University, 1999.

Makdisi, George, *The Rise of Colleges: Institutions of Learning in Islam and the West*, Edinburgh, Edinburgh University Press, 1981.

McClellan, James E. III, *Science Reorganized*, New York, Columbia University Press, 1983.

Meyerhof, Max, *Ten Treatises on the Eye Ascribed to Huain Ibn Ishaq*, Cairo, Government Press, 1928.

Meyerhof, Max, Von Aleandrien nach Bagdad, *Ein Beitrag zur Geschichte des philosophischen und medizinischen Unterrichts dei den Arabern*, Berlin, Verlag der Akademie der Wissenschaften, 1930.

Muhakqiq, Mahdi, "Risalet Hunayn Ibn Ishaq", *The Book of collection of Papers delivered on the 1200th Anniversary of the Foundation of Bayt al-Hikma*, edited by Bayt al-Hikma al-Abbasi: A'rakat al-Madi ve Ru'yat al-Hadır, Baghdad, Bayt al-Hikma Institution Publishing, Vol. 2, 2001.

Naji, Abd al-Jabbar, *Bayt al-Hikma al Baghdadi*, Baghdad, 2008.

Nöldeke, Theodor, *Die Erzahlun von Mausekönig und senien Ministern*, Göttingen, Dieterich'sche Verlags-Buchhandlung, 1879.

O'Leary, De Lacy, *How Greek Science Passed to the Arabs*, Goodword Books, 2002.

Peters, Francis, E., *The Harvest of Hellenism. A History of the Near East from Alexander the Great to the Triumph of Christianity*, New York, Simon & Shuster, 1972.

Pinto, Olga, "Al-Fath b. Khakan", *Encyclopaedia of Islam*, 2nd Edition, Vol. II, Leiden, Brill, 1960.

Rahman, Habib Ur, *A Chronology of Islamic History, 570–1000 CE*, London, T.a-Ha Publishers, 1994.

Rifa'i, Ahmad Ferid, *'Asr al-Ma'mun*, Cairo, Dar al-kutub al-Mısriyye, 1928.

Rosenthal, Franz, "From Arabic Books and manuscripts, XVI: As-Sarakhsi (?) on the Appropriate Behavior for Kings"; *Journal of the American Oriental Society*, Vol. 115, 1995, pp. 105–109.

Sayılı, Aydın, "Gondeshapur", *Encyclopedia of Islam*, 2nd Edition, Leiden, BRILL, 1965.

Sayılı, Aydın, "The Institutions of Science and Learning in the Muslim World", Ph.D. Thesis, Harvard University, Department of the History of Science and Learning, 1941.

Sayılı, Aydın, *Observatory in Islam and Its Place in the General History of the Observatory*, Ankara, Türk Tarih Kurumu, 1988.

Schoeler, Gregor, *Arabische Handschriften*, Tell II, Stutgart F. Steiner, 1990.

Shaki, Mansour, "The Denkard Account of History of the Zoroastrian Scriptures", *Archiv Orientalni, Praha*, Vol. 49, 1981, pp. 114–125.

Siassi, Ali Akbar, "L'Université de Gond-i Shapur et l'etendue de son rayonement", *Mélanges d'orientalisme offerts a Henri Massé*, edited by Anawati, G. C., Arberry, A. J., Bailey, H. W., et al., Téhéran, Imprimerie de L'Université, pp. 35–62, 1963.

Sourdel, Dominique, *Le Vizarat Abbaside*, Damas, 1959.

Sourdel, Dominique, "Bayt al-Hikma", *Encyclopedia of Islam*, 2nd Edition, Leiden, BRILL, 1960.

Steinschneider, Moritz, "Die arabischen Uebersetzungen aus dem Griechischen", *Zeitschrift der Deutschen Morgenländischen Gesellschaft*, Vol. 50, No. 2, 1896, Harrassowitz Verlag.

Totah, Khalil, *Al-Tarbiya 'Ind Al-Arab*, Jerusalem, 1933.

Totah, Khalil, *The Contribution of the Arabs to Education*, New York, Teachers College, Columbia University, 1926.

Watt, William Montgomery, *A Short History of Islam*, Oxford, One World Publication, 1996.

Wiet, Gaston, "Barbā", in *Encyclopedia of Islam*, 2nd Edition, Leiden, Brill, 2012.

Wüstenfeld, Ferdinand, *Die Academien Der Araber und Ihre Lehrer*, Göttingen, Vanderhoeck und Ruprecht, 1837.

Yücesoy, Hayrettin, *The Messianic Beliefs & Imperial Politics in Medieval Islam, The Abbasid Caliphate in the Early Ninth Century*, Columbia, The University of South Carolina Press, 2009.

Zou'bi, Moneed Rafe', Mohd Hazim Shah, *Science Institutionalization in Early Islam*, Amman, DAR Publisher, The University of Jordan, 2015.

Index

Abbas, Sundus 20
Abbasid: bureaucracy 2, 62; caliphate 1, 4, 37, 69; caliphs 1, 2, 3, 6, 9, 11, 15, 20, 22, 28, 36, 39, 40, 56, 63, 65, 66, 68, 70, 74; court 11, 16, 25, 39, 46, 62, 72; culture/cultural life 4, 61; dynasty 3; Empire 1, 8; era/period/epoch 4, 5, 9, 10, 15, 25, 28, 30, 32, 35, 37, 39, 43, 47, 59, 64, 80; intellectuals 72; life 5; literary works 22; society 2, 74
Abd al-Aziz al-Kinani 51, 52, 54, 69
Abd al-Hakem Ibn Amr bin Abid Allah Ibn Safwan al-Jamhî 35
Abd al-Muttalib Ibn Hisham (the grandfather of prophet Mohamad) 27
Abu al-Faraj al-Isfahani 34
Abu al-Fida / Abulfeda 42, 68
Abu Hassan 26, 62
Abu Ma'shar Ibn Muhammed Ibn 'Umar al-Balkhi (Albo Masar) 45
Abu Sahl [al-Fadl] Ibn Nawbakht 46, 57, 78
Abu'l Hasan Ali bin Razin 65
Abyssinians 27
Academia dei Lincei of Rome 22
Adam 57
'Adud al-Dawla, Buyid ruler of Fars 58
Ahmad Ibn Hanbal 7, 74
Alexander the Great 1
Alexandria 11, 17
Alexandria Library 47
Alexandria Museum 10, 18, 41

Ali bin Ahmed al-Imrani 37
Ali bin Yahya al-Munajjim 31, 36, 72, 73
Allan Ibn Hassan al-Warraq /Allan al-Shu'ubi 26, 54
Amin ala al-Tarjama (secretary of translations) 19, 28, 30
Amsar (garrison towns) 2
Amuriye (Amorium) 59
Ankara 59
Antioch 11
Anusharwan / Khusrav I., Sassanian King 42, 53
Arabian Nights 5
Arabic 1, 2, 3, 4, 5, 14, 16, 17, 18, 19, 20, 21, 28, 29, 34, 58, 73; civilization 16; culture 3, 43; manuscripts 14; poetry 3, 58; sources/ literature 4, 5, 14, 16, 41, 42, 51
Arabs 2, 3, 19, 22, 27, 28, 34, 41, 43, 57, 65
Aramaic 1
Aristotle 42, 43, 53, 62, 63
al-Asma'i 56, 57, 79
Assyrians 21
Astrologer 5, 19, 20, 45, 46, 50, 72, 73, 80
Astromancy 5
Astronomer 27, 31, 45, 46, 73, 78, 79, 80
Astronomy 3, 5, 16, 21, 31, 32, 39
Atatürk 75
Athens 10, 11, 41, 42
Avicenna 58

Index

Babylonians 21
Badawi, Abd al-Rahman 53
Baghdad 1, 2, 3, 4, 5, 9, 10, 15, 16, 17, 18, 20, 21, 25, 28, 29, 35, 41, 51, 54, 59, 60, 69, 70, 71, 72
al-Balazuri 34
Balkh 2, 45
Balty-Gueston, Marie Genevieve 52, 54
Banu Musa brothers / Banu Musa al-Munajjim (sons of Musa Ibn Shakir the astronomer) Muhammad, Ahmad, and al-Hasan 29, 30, 31, 61
Barmakid family 2, 26, 64
Bayt al-Suwar al-Mudhahhabe 53
Bayt al-Zahab 53
Berlin Academy 16
Bimaristan (shifakhane-hospital) 11, 29
al-Biruni 41
Bishr al-Marisi 35, 51, 69
Bladel, Kevin Van 44
Bologna University 16
Brockelmann, Carl 15, 16, 18
Buddhist priesthoods 2
al-Buhturi, the Jurist Judge 57
Buzoe 42
Buzurgmihr 65
Byzantine: book collections 41; country/lands 59, 60; emperor 39, 59, 60, 63; philosophers 53
Byzantium 62, 63, 64, 73

Cairo 10, 17, 70, 72
Caliph of God (Khalifat Allah) 7
Cambridge University 16
Central Asia 1, 2
Chinese Tang Dynasty 4
Christian, philosophy and science 11
Columbia University 16
Createdness of Qur'an 7, 10, 50, 51, 52, 65, 68, 69, 74
Cyprus 60, 63

Dahhak Ibn Qay 46
Damascus 1, 6, 18, 51, 70
Demirci, Mustafa 20
Dhouban 57
al-Dinawari 6

Eche, Yusuf 19, 21, 35, 41, 43, 47, 50, 51, 54, 68, 69, 74, 75, 76
Egypt 1, 46
Egyptian University 17
epistemological: dichotomy 75; models/structure 4, 6
Euclid 39, 59
Europe 16, 22
European: academy 14, 16, 17, 18; languages 14, 15

Fath Ibn Khaqan 37
Fatimid: Caliphs 7, 11; institute of learning 72
Fatma bint Sharik al-Ansariyya 34
Federico Cesi, Italian aristocrat 22
Flügel, Güstav 14

Galen 28, 29, 30, 70
geometry 3, 5, 31, 73
Golden Age of the Islamic civilization see Islamic civilization
Goldziher, Ignaz 75, 76
grammar 5, 32, 60
Greco: Arabic translation movement 62, 37; Byzantine elements/sources 1, 53
Greek 28, 29, 41, 79; -books/texts/ sources 9, 11, 14, 18, 28, 30, 36, 53, 59, 60, 61, 62, 63, 64; classics 3; intellectual heritage 2; philosophy/ philosophers 6, 7, 11, 41, 42, 52, 53, 60; science 11, 69
Greeks 41, 42, 43
Gutas, Dimitri 43, 44, 45, 47, 61, 62, 63, 74, 76

Hadith (prophetic traditions) 4, 7, 35
al-Hajjaj, Ibn Matar 60, 63
al-Hamawi, Yaqut 73
Hamza al-Isfahani 43, 44, 65, 69
Harun al-Rashid, Caliph 2, 9, 21, 22, 25, 26, 39, 40, 46, 47, 56, 58, 59, 64, 70, 72, 78
Harvard University 75
Haykel al-Rukham 53
Hellenic Athenian institutions of learning 10
Hellenistic 3, 4, 53
Hindu 11

al-hikma/wisdom *see* philosophical
  sciences
Himyarite letters 27
Hippocrates 28
Hira 28
historiography 9, 14
Hitti, Phillip 18
Holy Ka'ba 35
Hubaysh Ibn al-Hasan 73
Hulagu, Ilkhanate Ruler 21
Hunayn Ibn Ishaq 17, 18, 28, 29, 41,
  52, 64, 70, 73

Ibn Abi Usaibia/ Ibn Abi Usaybia
  25, 28
Ibn al-Batriq 60, 63
Ibn al-Farra 60, 61
Ibn Ali Al-Haryish 26
Ibn al-Ibri, Bar Hebraeus 25, 31
Ibn al-Muqa'fa 42, 43
Ibn al-Qufti 25, 26, 59
Ibn 'Asakir 34
Ibn Hawqal 41, 42
Ibn Hazım al-Andalusi 35
Ibn Juhul 25
Ibn Nubata al-Masri 60
Ibn Schobba 15
Ibn Taghribirdi 50, 68, 69
Ilkhanate Mongols 70
Imam al-Huda 7
India 1, 3, 42
Indian: kings 43; language 36;
  philosophers 53; sources 3, 9
Iranian: bureaucrats 43; language 44,
  45; literature 3
Iraq 21
Ishaq Ibn Ibrahim al-Mouslabi 31
Islamic: civilization 7, 76; culture and
  community 7, 15; Hellenism 11;
  identity 3; Ottoman civilization 76;
  religion 2; sciences 5; society 74;
  tradition 4, 21; university 20, 31
Isma'ili: fiqh/doctrine 7;
  propaganda 8
İwan (hall) 51, 52

al-Jahiz 57, 58, 72, 79
Jewish philosophy and science 11
Jundishapur/Gundaysabur/
  Gondeshapur 11, 29

Katib Çelebi 14, 15
Kazakhstan 4
Khalid al-Barmaki 2

al-Khalili, Jim 22, 23
Khedr, Ahmed Attallah 20
Khurasan 2
al-Khwarizmi *see* Mohammed bin
  Musa al-Khwarizmi
King Luqianus 53

Lapidus, Ira M. 2, 28
Leibniz 16
logic 5, 39
Lyceum 42
Lyons, Jonathan 22

Madinat al-Salam (the city of peace)
  see Baghdad
al-Mahdi, Caliph 2
Makdisi, George 75, 76
Mamluk era 50, 68
al-Ma'mun, Caliph 6, 7, 9, 10, 11, 15,
  16, 17, 18, 23, 26, 27, 28, 29, 30, 31,
  32, 35, 37, 39, 40, 44, 50, 51, 54, 56,
  57, 58, 59, 60, 61, 62, 63, 64, 66, 67,
  68, 69, 70, 71, 72, 73, 74, 78, 79
al-Maqrizi 41, 47
Marwan I, Ibn al-Hakam, Umayyad
  Caliph 34, 35
Masarjawaih 35
al-Masudi 35, 39
mathematics/arithmetic/algebra 3, 5,
  16, 31, 32, 73
Mawali 1
medicine 3, 5, 11, 21, 28, 31, 72, 73
Medina 1
Merv 6
Meyerhof, Max 17, 18, 28, 29, 30, 69
Middle East 2, 4
Mihna/inquisition/ordeal 6, 7, 66, 68,
  69, 73, 74
Mohamed Ibn Ali bin Ali bin
  Ibrahim bin Ahmed bin Mohamed
  al-Ansari 53
Mohammed bin Jubayr bin Mut'am
  34
Mohammed bin Musa al-Khwarizmi
  27
Mongol invasion 5, 70, 71

Mt. Qaysun 18
Mu'awiyya, Caliph 35, 65
al-Mu'tadid, Caliph 9
al-Mu'tamid, Caliph 36, 46
Mu'tazila 7, 50, 54, 65, 71, 74
Muhammad, Prophet 27, 35
Muhammed bin al-Haris al-Tha'labi 65
Muhammed bin Musa 29
al-Muqaddisi 58
Musa bin Shakir 31, 79
Muslim: institutions of learning 6; scholars 4, 6, 75; society 54; world 4
al-Musta'sim, Caliph 70
al-Mutawakkil, Caliph 7, 17, 18, 28, 29, 36, 37, 66, 69, 71, 72, 73, 74

al-Nadim 9, 10, 14, 25, 26, 27, 28, 36, 39, 40, 41, 44, 45, 46, 59, 62, 63, 64, 70, 78, 79, 80
Naji, Abd al-Jabbar 21
Neo-Platonists 11
Nestorian: Christians 2, 28; translators 72
Noah 57
nomadic culture 2

O'Leary, De Lacy 69
Osman bin Said al-Darimi 35
Osman, Caliph 34
Ottoman: culture 15; epoch 6; realm 76
Oxford University 16

Pahlavi 42, 43, 44, 45
papermaking 4
Paris 75; Academy 16; University 16
patronage 4, 6, 8, 16, 20, 21, 25, 30, 31, 50, 59, 60, 61, 64, 78
Persia 46
Persian: Adab 4; culture 1; kings 22, 44, 45; language 11, 15, 41, 43, 45, 47, 64, 79; philosophers 53
philosophical sciences 4, 6, 10, 32, 52, 65, 66, 71
Plato 43, 53
Prague University 16

pre-Islamic: Arabic language 34; Arabic poetry 3; civilization 41; heritage 37; institutions 41; life 34; sciences 45, 47, 59, 68
Prussian Court 16
Ptolemaic institutions of learning 10
Ptolemy 26, 62, 64

Qadi al-Nu'man 7
al-Qalqashandi 70, 71
al-Qayrawani 57
al-Qifti 14, 31, 25, 26, 59, 64, 79
Quraishi traditions 34
Qur'an 5, 7, 10, 32, 50, 51, 52, 57, 65, 68, 69, 74
Qur'anic exegesis 4

Raqqa 30
Rifa'i, Ahmad Farid 16
Rome 22, 41

Saddam Husain 21
Sa'id al-Andalusi 39, 50
Said Ibn Huraym al-Katib as Sharik of Sahl Ibn Harun 26
Sâlm /Sahib/head of 14, 17, 26, 40, 60, 65, 78
Sam, son of Noah 57
Samarkand 4
Samarra 69
Sarton, George 11, 76
Sassanian: realm 11; sources 9
Sassanid: imperial ideology 43, 62; institutions of learning 10; royal libraries 47
Sayılı, Aydın 32, 75, 76
Schoeler, Gregor 44
Shaki, M. 44
Shamsiyah observatory 16, 18
Shi'ite: concept of Imamate 4; fiqh 7
Shu'ubizm (Shu'ubiyya) 54
Sind ibn 'Ali 18
Sirdab al-Muluk 53
Steinschneider, Moritz 14, 15
al-Subki 52
Sumerians 21
Sunni Islam 8, 74
Syria 75

Syriac 3, 9, 11, 17, 25, 28, 29, 30, 36, 64

Tafsir 32
Talas Battle 4, 72
Taraz 4
Thabit Ibn Qurra 30, 73
theology 4, 5, 6, 50, 51
Tigris 21
Toderini, Giambattista 15
Totah, Khalil 16, 17, 18
Turkey, Republic of 75
Turkish: culture 1; experience of modernization 76; royal family 72

Ullmann, Manfred 37
al-'ulum al'aqliyya (rational or intellectual sciences) 4
'ulum al-'awa'il (sciences of the ancients) 4, 5, 11, 42, 73, 74, 76
al-'ulum al-dakhila (foreign sciences) 4, 5, 9, 35, 36

al-'ulum al-falsafiyya *see* philosophical sciences
al-'ulum al-hikamiyya *see* philosophical sciences
Umayyads 2
UNESCO 21

al-Wathiq, Caliph 29, 65, 66, 69, 74
Western: civilization 22; Europe 76; readers/readership 22; scholars 75
westernization 76
Wüstenfeld, Ferdinand 15

Yahya bin Khalid bin Barmak, Harun al-Rashid's vizier 26, 62
Yahya ibn abi-Mansur 18, 72
Yuhanna bin al-Batriq 28, 60, 63
Yuhanna Ibn Masawayh 17, 18, 28, 29, 59

Zahirriyye Library 51
al-Zehebi 52

For Product Safety Concerns and Information please contact our EU representative GPSR@taylorandfrancis.com
Taylor & Francis Verlag GmbH, Kaufingerstraße 24, 80331 München, Germany

www.ingramcontent.com/pod-product-compliance
Lightning Source LLC
Chambersburg PA
CBHW051757230426
43670CB00012B/2331